WHEEL&DEAL

GINGKO PRESS

FORE WORD

With rising rental costs and changing trends, retail outlets and brands are facing tough challenges needing to balance their books while speculating on the success of their new products. In recent years, temporary and mobile establishments have grown in number in response to these forces, despite the fact that not so long ago pop-up shops were seen as a passing fad. On the contrary, pop-up businesses are everywhere, as brands begin to recognize the benefits of a mobile footprint in today's retail industry.

As mobile establishments are always on the move, the rent is drastically lower or even non-existent as compared to that of a permanent shop space. Simply wheel to an event, set up shop and wheel away at the end of the business day.

Governments have also been promoting entrepreneurship, which comes as a great benefit to businesses whose funds are tight. Having an option to move to another location to increase profits will definitely appeal to new business owners. In addition, as there are no long-term commitments, the brand can better react to market forces and make changes to business and marketing plans. For example, opening up a temporary shop during peak seasons and moving or closing it down during the quiet months. For brands that do not have a brick and mortar shop, a pop-up mobile establishment gives the brand a physical presence and a way to interact with their customers face-to-face.

Mobile businesses can generate a significant amount of buzz, drawing attention and crowds as they appear suddenly in a given location. Imagine a container truck store or bicycle coffee shop popping up out of nowhere, people will definitely be intrigued by their appearance. A unique setup could also generate publicity for an event, especially when it is the launch of a new product, service or business idea. Such experimentation help brands to gauge the success of a new product and engage with their target audience.

Another advantage over brick and mortar shops is their temporality. Since pop-up mobile establishments only exist in a given location for a limited time, it creates a sense of urgency for customers who wish to purchase the product or service. Unlike a permanent store, customers must purchase now or regret when the pop-up is gone. More often than not, these mobile businesses develop a cult following, with fans following them from location to location.

Not limited to commerce or marketing, some artists have also adopted the use of mobile establishments due to their low cost and high mobility, using them for artistic purposes or social commentary. As these mobile installations are eye-catching and generate lots of hype, artists have the opportunity to engage a larger public with their art — whether for its own sake, or to address social concerns. Some designers also experiment with new concepts in sales and marketing as they introduce or reinvent products in an utterly unique arena.

As pop-up businesses come and go, *Wheel and Deal* aims to compile the breadth of these design and marketing efforts, highlighting new ideas and concepts in mobility with the best of commerce on wheels. Designed around the concept of vehicle license and registration plates, *Wheel and Deal* is divided into 5 chapters, each categorized by the size of these establishments and the mode of their transport, much like the system used in standard vehicle classification. *Cart Away* showcases push-carts as well as any mobile businesses that can be pushed by human strength; *Two Wheelers* reveals the ingenious ways companies and artists have utilized the humble bicycle; *Four Wheel Drive* powers the humble automobile with unique effects; *Next Stop* charts the way public transportation has been used to market and promote brands; and lastly, *Keep on Trucking* features trailers and food trucks that have transported the best design concepts and retail efforts into our neighborhoods.

Illustrated throughout with plans, conceptual art and photography, *Wheel and Deal* captures the best mobile business concepts of recent years permanently in a book. Grab it before it moves on!

CONTENTS

CHAPTER

01

CART
AWAY

FACE-O-MAT

—

Designer
Tobias Gutmann

—

Tobias Gutmann is an illustrator, storyteller, artist and sometimes a graphic designer but mostly a nice guy. This peculiar artist, has been travelling around the globe since late 2013 with the intention of creating abstract portraits of people.

In total, he has travelled 25,000 miles with his portable analogue portrait booth, known as the Face-o-mat, stopping in cities like Stockholm, Milan, Dar es Salaam, Tokyo and London.

The Face-o-mat is a very special machine. First, the customer takes a seat in front of a small photo booth type window. He then adjusts some levers to configure the outcome of the portrait, ranging from colour, black or white, facelift, classical or avant-garde. Afterwards, and for a small fee, Gutmann creates the portrait in three minutes. The portraits are abstract representations of the models, much like the rest of Gutmann's work and illustrations.

The entire procedure takes place in the portable booth he has designed and built, equipped with simple mechanisms that make the costumer's experience even more pleasing and amusing. The Face-o-mat is normally customized to match the language and the context where it is set up, making the experience even more familiar and context specific.

FOLD INN

—

Designer
Lieke Jildou de Jong,
Alei Verspoor, Aliki van der Kruijs

Photographer
Carina Hesper

—

Fold Inn is a box that unfolds into a bedroom.
It offers a temporary room to stay within
larger or vacant spaces. Fold Inn is developed for people that need to work and stay at
diffrent places, such as business people and
expats. When folded, the box leaves space
for workplaces, conferences, presentations or
other work-related activities.

Fold Inn is designed to be set up quickly and
it is simple to assemble. It fits in a standard
elevator and can be moved around with
attached wheels.

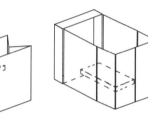

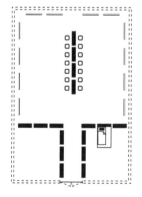

Fold Inn is folded out, the space
is being used to stay the night.

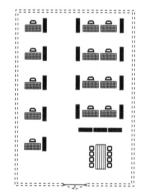

Fold inn is folded in and the
space can be used to work

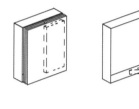

Fold Inn is folded in, the space is
being used for an exhibition

fold Inn, folded out   fold Inn, folded in   chair   desk   meeting table   art

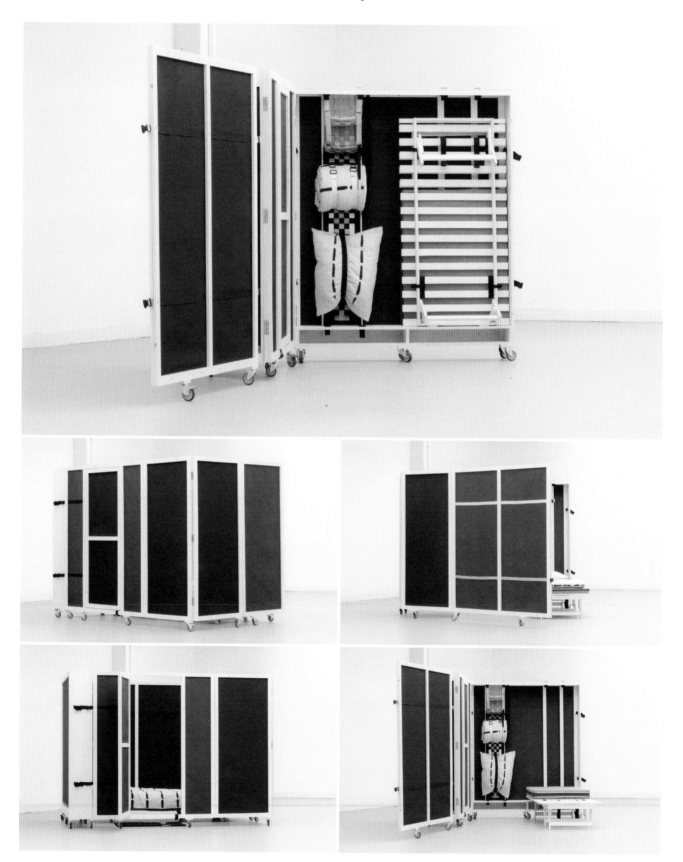

Cart Away

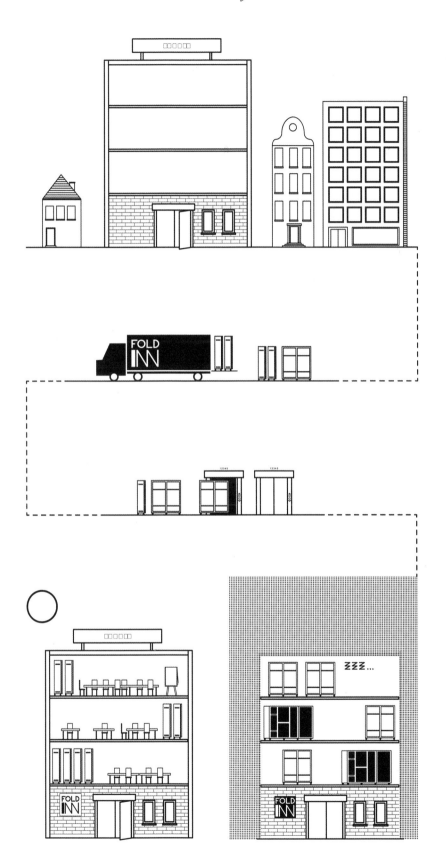

015

COS POP-UP STORE

—

Designer
chmara.rosinke conceptional design

Photographer
chmara.rosinke

—

A pop-up store for the fashion brand COS. Based on the concept of mobile hospitality, we were commissioned to design a pop-up fashion presentation tool. Functions, colours and the aesthetical approach were adapted to the needs of the fashion label.

DIY SERVICE WAGON

—

Designer
chmara.rosinke conceptional design

Photographer
chmara.rosinke

—

The vertical kitchen is a contemporary re-interpretation of the "service-wagon" by Ferdinand Kramer from 1941. Contrary to the Krammers project, we have ordered the functions vertically to improve the usability. This version is easier to move and turn, and it fits in every elevator. "DIY service wagon" was realized for the exhibition "Nomadic Furniture 3.0. New Liberated Living?" at MAK-Österreichisches Museum für ange-wandte Kunst / Gegenwartskunst in 2013.

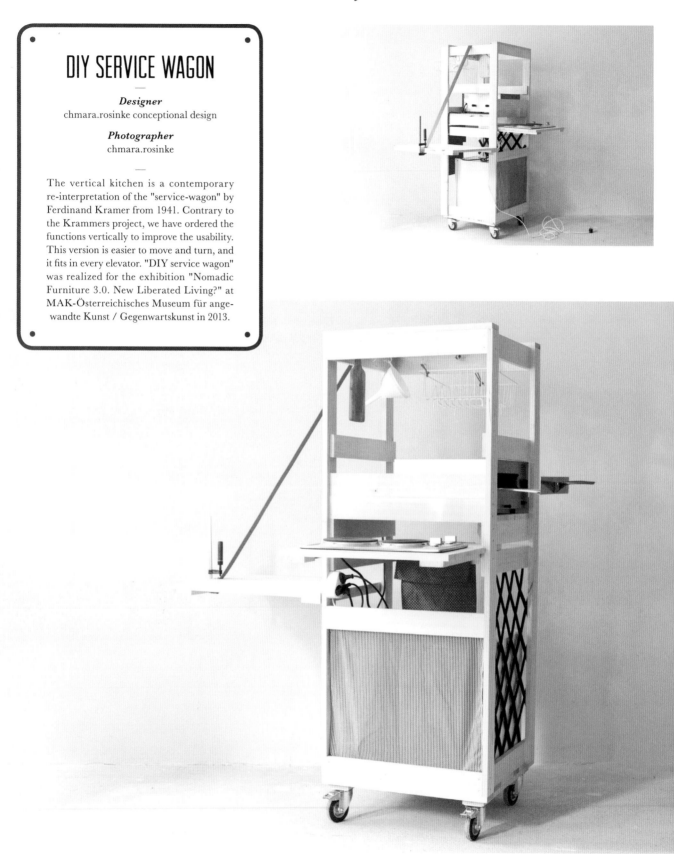

IL CARRELLO

—

Designer
Ciszak Dalmas

Photographer
Ciszak Dalmas

—

Il Carrello serves as a stylish and adaptable way to display various things, such as books and magazines, fashion accessories, plants and flowers, glasses and kitchen utensils. It can be used as a display or auxiliary storage in restaurants, cafes, catering, shops, and also as part of a window display. The structure is deliberately open to encourage multiple usage. In addition, the ever growing range of accessories opens up new possibilities of storage, display or organisation. It is made from Birch plywood laminated with different colours, and produced using CNC manufacturing. Also it has been designed to pack flat into a very small box. Il Carrello is produced by La Clinica Design.

THE WAVE

—

Designer
Bureau Detours

Photographer
Bureau Detours La Familia

—

New Danish parks are often designed for specific male dominated activities such as parkour and skating, leaving the girls to watch the activities or go shop in the malls. It is a rude generalization, but still there is a big need to research what girls think of the public spaces and learn what we can do to create more girl-friendly public spaces.

In cooperation with teenage girls in Hillerød, Bureau Detours designed and built a handcart named The Wave. The Wave is designed for the girls' need to have a mobile sitting area that can be moved by hand to quiet surroundings or festive events. In the cart there is space for storing cushions, blankets, umbrellas and a sound system. The project is part of a regional project with Kulturmetropol Øresund and seven other municipalities in Denmark.

CARREM

—

Designer
Andreu Carulla studio

Photographer
Andreu Carulla studio

—

CarRem is a couple of carts designed to hold food and drinks, and seasonings, together with the Tamborem stool, and belongs to the Retro Sports Furniture collection. The goal is that restaurant guests can choose the herb they prefer right from the plant and enjoy its flavour and aroma in the freshest way possible.

The cocktail model holds a couple of ice buckets as well as two plant pots for different herbs to enrich a drink, whereas the food model holds five plant pots for different aromatic herbs to complement the dishes.

With a minimalistic aesthetic, it has a minor impact on the ambience, its glass surface leads to a floating sensation of the elements placed above. It also provides mobility thanks to its wheelbarrow structure, so it can be easily handled in small spaces.

Its handlebars are made of antique rowing paddles which provide good stability to the whole cart, and its tubes are painted in medal colours (gold, silver and bronze).

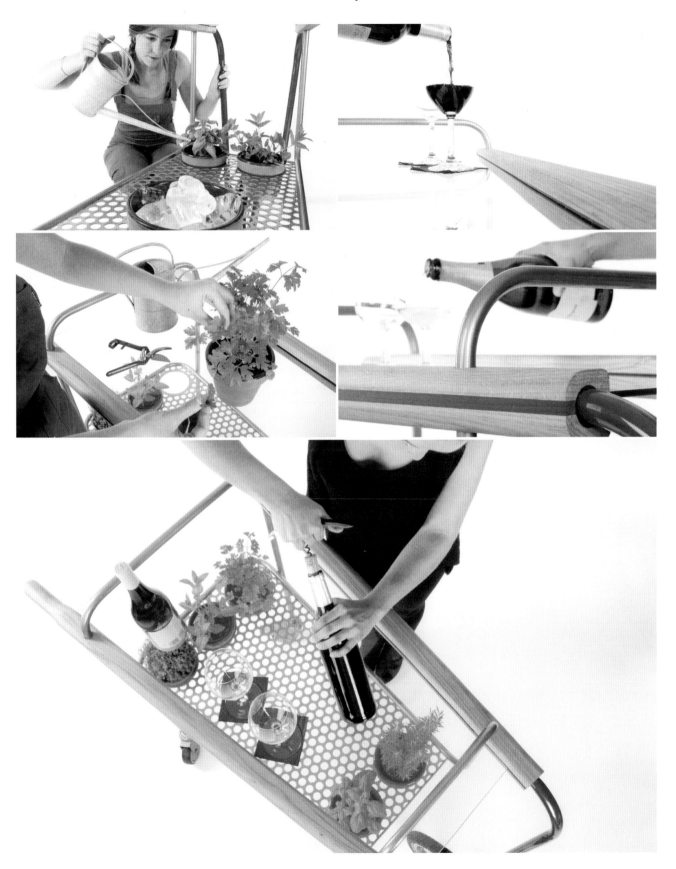

SMART CHEESE CART FOR BEEMSTER CHEESE

Studio
Studiomfd

Photographer
Johannes van Assem

Designer
Martijn Frank Dirks

Collaboration
Young Perfect Promotions, Spinder interior builders

De Beemster is the name of a very special and authentic 17th-century polder in the Netherlands. Young Perfect Promotions hired studiomfd to make a design to activate the Beemster cheese brand in retail.

Studiomfd designed a picturesque market stand that invites shoppers to stop a moment and savour a nice piece of Beemster cheese. A trolley-stand that looks rural and authentic with a contemporary twist, thus fitting in seamlessly with the recent rebranding of the brand.

The design is colour-themed. The milk pails and wheels, based on an old-fashioned transport bicycle, are painted Beemster blue. The covering tarpaulin is printed in the brand's colours. It creates an oasis of atmosphere in the usually rather functional supermarket environment. With some peace and quiet, the stand invites visitors to enjoy the taste of good cheese in a setting that is true to the culture of the Beemster brand.

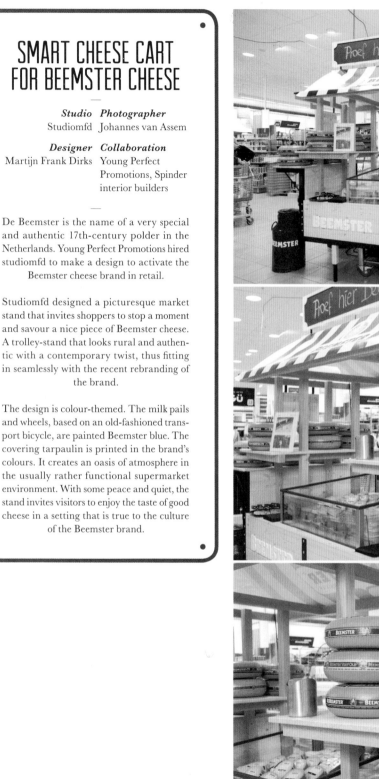

Beemster Kaas Young Perfect Shopper Activation

UNICORN

—

Designer
Brosmind

Photographer
Mertixell Arjalaguer

—

This sculpture is part of our personal project "What's Inside?", released in June 2013, in which we reflected about how things work and what they hide inside. To do so, we developed 20 different detailed illustrations, a series of photographs and this dissected unicorn that we built from scratch at our studio. All the shapes inside are hand-painted, and upon pressing a button, the sculpture starts to swing hypnotically.

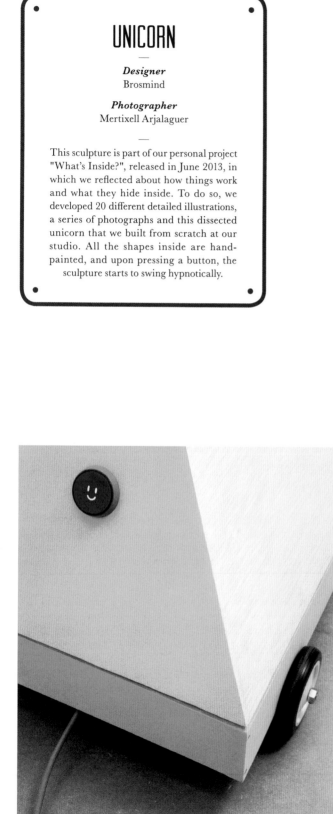

DRI DRI AT KENSINGTON MALL

—

Designer
elips design

Photographer
Carlo Carossio

Dri Dri sets up a pop up shop again, this time in the Kensington Shopping Mall in High Street Kensington tube station. Using as much of the previous installation as possible, we created the feel of the Italian beach with sunny colours. The beach houses divide the space, creating an hidden area, and the umbrellas, sea and sun on the wall simulate the scenery of a beach.

CARRO PER APERITIVI

—

Designer
Ciszak Dalmas

Photographer
Ciszak Dalmas

—

This cart for a cheese display is an evolution of "Il Carrello" since it was customized for a specific restaurant. It is produced in Oak wood and painted with a light blue finish.

MIXI MICROCREAMERY

Studio
Breakaway Innovation Group (BIG)

Creative Director and Writer
Scott Maney

Designer and Illustrator
Heather Crosby

Designer
Andrew Sithimorada

Branding of the state-of-the-art vending machine that creates fresh, custom, hard-packed ice cream. Mixi celebrates the Willy Wonka nature of such a contraption and makes it fun and memorable, with an image far from traditional creamery.

MERRY-GO-ROUND

—

Designer
Nuno Pimenta

Festival
Walk&Talk Azores - Public Art Festival

Photographer
Nuno Pimenta, Rui Soares

—

Merry-Go-Round is an urban device that subverts one of the greatest symbols of a consumerist society (the shopping cart), subconsciously leading the user to a carousel—a place of joy and fun (merry-go-round).

By counteracting the freedom of movement that normally characterizes these carts (ironically moving in circles), we are reminded that consumerism does not take us anywhere. Or in the best case scenario, to the starting point.

AGNES THE TYPO TRUCK

—

Designer
Old School New School
Design and Typography

Photographer
Veronica Grow

Collaboration
Kitty Lo

—

Agnes the Typo Truck is a gracious old fashioned lady who is a type and lettering purist. When she hits the streets, magic happens. She is like a magnet, and people are enchanted by her fine livery and lovely sign-painted exterior. Once upon a time, Agnes and her lover Percy were a dashing couple who used to have lovers tiffs over their different affections for Bodoni and Didot. They used to travel the streets together, and love showing the world their passion for type. Then, one sad day in 1985, Percy dumped Agnes for the younger model, known as "the keyboard."

A speculative side project for both Old School Press (the OSNS Professional Design Studio) and our students, this real world project helped students discover the power that they have as storytellers and designers to touch people's hearts through innovative non-traditional means (not posters), as well as fresh ways to influence behavior and create change via social engagement.

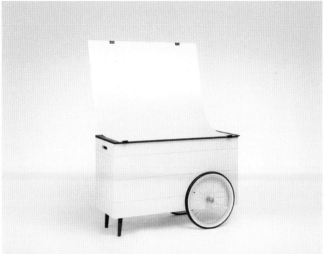

TEATRINO NEGRINI

—

Designer
Ciszak Dalmas

Photographer
Ciszak Dalmas

—

Il Carrello can trace it roots back to the Teatrino Negrini, a prototype display cart for Negrini, an export company of Italian food products. The idea resulted from the need of high quality pictures of the products without overspending on still-life photo features. It consists of a box containing a complete photo set, and its use is combined with a series of basic photography training held within the company.

MOBILE URBAN SQUARE

—

Designer
Izmo

Photographer
garu-garu for Izmo

—

The Mobile Urban Square installation is the result of the self-built design workshop organized by Izmo within the Progetto Leonia, a research and training program aimed at disseminating the practices of reuse in the field of urban regeneration. The project regarded the theoretical and design processes and focused on the spreading of reuse and self-construction in order to achieve a multifunctional mobile installation (3×2 metres—about the size of a parking lot) to be placed as a urban furniture in the district of Porta Palazzo in Turin.

CINCAI

—

Designer
Cheong Zhi Ying,
Ngew Keat Seng, Swee Pei Foong

Photographer
Cheong Wen Cong

Collaboration
Herbie Phoon

—

The meaning of this project is to explore the Malaysian living lifestyle "cincai" ("whatever" in English) and bring out the positive side of it. The Hokkien word "cincai" is widely used in Manglish and Singlish, and is derived from a Chinese word "秤採", describing an estimated deal with customers by using balance in the market. It is not 100% accurate but yet it lightens the workload and makes life simpler.

There are tons of choices out there in the market. Imagine the amount of time spent every time you try to decide what you want to eat. There are too many aspects to be taken into consideration: price, taste, convenience, nutrition and most of all, cravings. In fact, they are all the same, wrapped under different labels.

Here we got an idea which frees you from making a food decision. We are a group of students from Dasein Academy of Art, bringing you A "Cincai" Food Project.

青菜

CINCAI

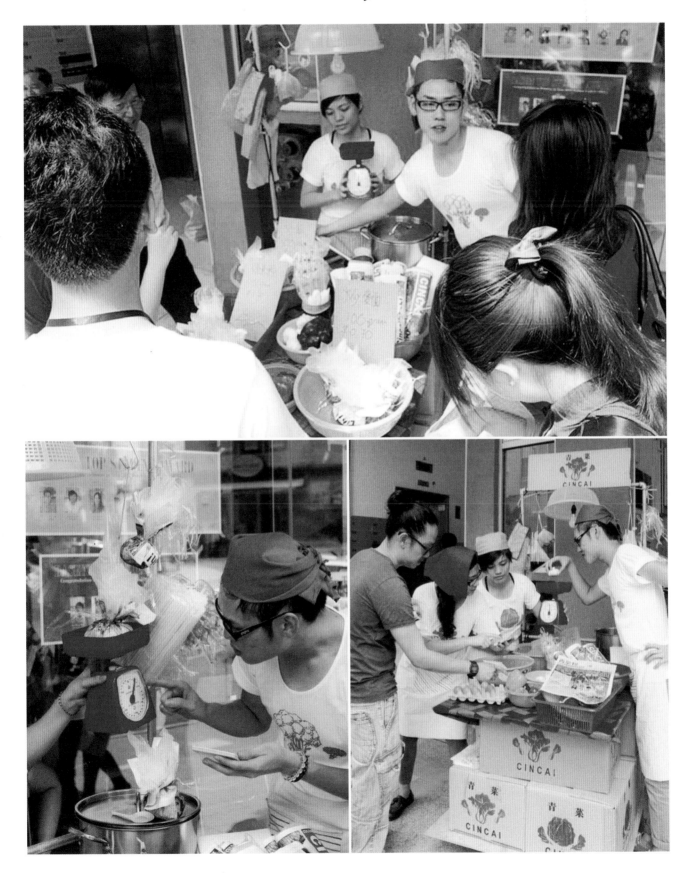

#AGRONAUTAS – NEW URBAN REALITIES

—

Design
Pezestudio

Photographer
Mariel Vidal - Doblimagen,
Juan Dopico and Pezestudio

—

The Agronautas platform has built different prototypes attending to different community needs, to socialize and share sustainable practices as well as to visualize and minimize energy and resources consumption. Also, it aims to bring sustainable innovation access to anyone and to adapt energy systems to different needs.

"Openlabs Towards Self Sufficiency" is proposed as a link between regulated research spaces and public spaces accessible to everyone to create open learning communities. It includes the processes of research and innovation through co-creation, exploration, experimentation and evaluation of innovative ideas to be tested in real situations. Urban and community agents are introduced as a source of creation. This allows direct evaluation and possible adoption by users.

WIND TURBINE
energy production
by wind force

RAINWATER
COLLECTION
wicker roof cover
and epdm sheet

12V ELECTRIC
CIRCUIT
energy storage for
lighting and
music

PARASITE
SOLAR OVEN
adaptable
to any window
(also for common
housing units)

BOTIJO COOLER
natural cooling by
evaporation and night
radiation

EARTHWORM
FILTER
grease filter

BIOPLANTER
macrophyte
water depuration

FOLDABLE
DOORS
cañizo, local
fiber

REMOVABLE
STRUCTURE
local wood

SUN
PROTECTION
curtains made of
natural fibers

ENERGY BIKE
human powered
energy production

MOBILE SYSTEM
wheeled
scaffolding
structure

BAERCK

—

Designer
llot llov

Photographer
Vera Hofmann

—

When creating the concept of the interior, the design studio llot llov immersed the concept of the open architecture already given by the space. In order to support a pure aesthetic, the wood used in the building process is left natural, but combined with white surfaces and mirrors. The aim is to create a light and elegant atmosphere with these simple and raw materials.

The mobility of the modules is an essential part of the concept, enabling a regular change in appearance through time. The inspiration for the modules come from various vehicles of different decades. The idea is that these vehicles transport the chosen items to BAERCK in Berlin. Each module is lead by a different inspiration, for example a droshky, an old Ford or an old truck. The style of the different labels and pieces are supported by the look of furniture.

ROCA ON WHEELS

—

Designer
Andreu Carulla studio

Photographer
Alicia G. Salzmann

—

Roca on Wheels is an interpretation of Roca's cuisine and style brought to the new dessert cart for El Celler de Can Roca.

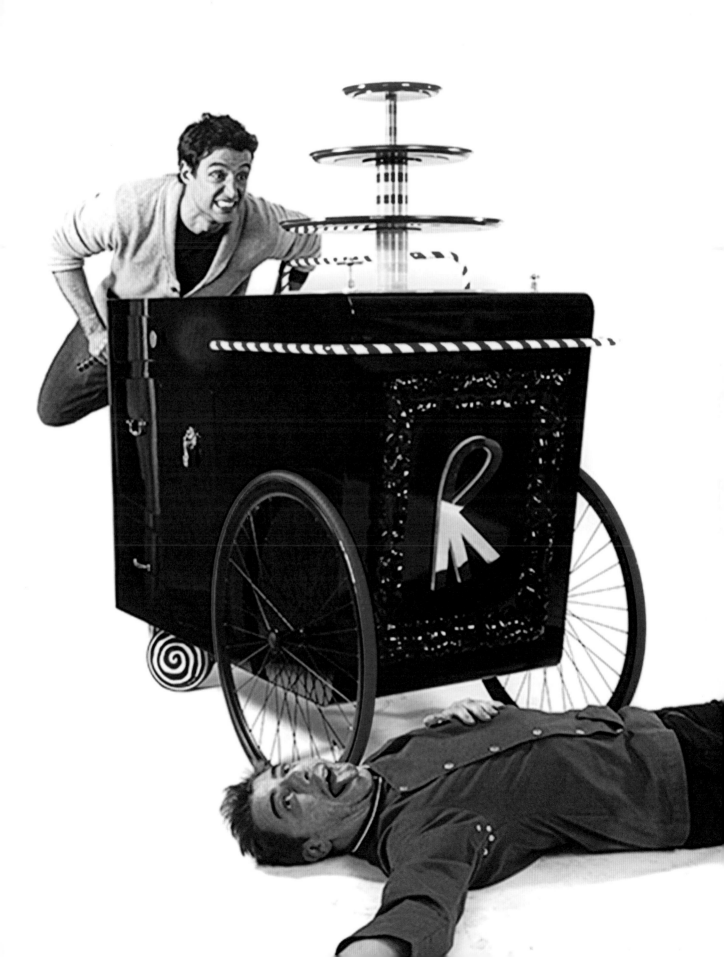

BEEBOX MOBILE WORKSPACE

—

Studio
Buro Beehive

Designer
Bart de Groot,
Christophe Veen

Photographer
Christophe Veen,
Thomas Born

—

The Beebox is a desk, as well as a lockable storage, acoustic panelling and dividing walls, all in one.

IJS SOLAR
ICE CREAM CART

—

Designers
Springtime Industrial Design

Partners
IJs & Zopie, Odenwald Organic

Photographer
Springtime

—

This innovative vending cart keeps ice cream cold by using solar energy. The photovoltaic panel in the roof charges the vehicle's batteries during the day, resulting in an energy neutral solution. This eliminates the need for an external power source. Even when the sun is not out, the batteries have plenty of capacity to supply the freezer with energy all day long. The cart plugs into any standard AC wall outlet to recharge the batteries overnight. The roof is elevated and lowered electrically. (www.solaricecreamcart.eu)

TV BARROW

—

Designer
CW&T

Photographer
CW&T

—

TV + Wheelbarrow = TV barrow

We love watching movies in bed, but we also love watching stuff in the living room. To fulfill both loves, we built a wheelbarrow for our screen so we could easily move it around and maneuver up and down small steps.

The 700c road bike wheel is attached to a bicycle fork. The rest of the parts are machined aluminum connections that fit around standard 1 inch aluminum tubes. Each component is secured with set screws so the legs are collapsible and the tilt of the screen is adjustable.

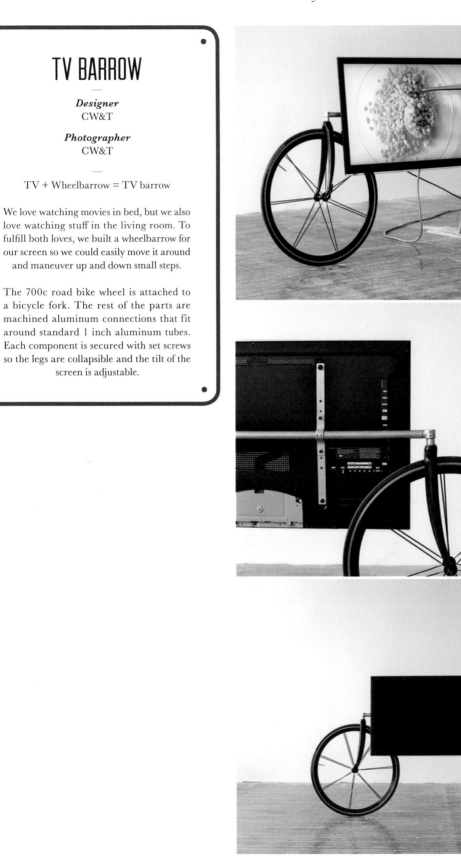

ONE-SQM-HOUSE

—

Designer
Van Bo Le-Mentzel

Photographer
Daniela Gellner Lorber

—

The smallest house in the world, it measures 80cm×100cm with a height of 200cm. To sleep in it, just flip it to the side.

People in the USA and Austria have built it mostly for private use or just to make a signage in public spaces. You can transport it via Bus or Metro thanks to its four wheels. A New Zealand backpacker used it to open a coffeeshop—and it is probably the smallest in the world.

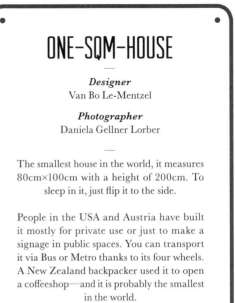

LOG BENCH

Design
Stefano Sciullo

Photographer
Indaco Biazzo

Collaboration
Caplavur

The Log Bench was born to live comfortably in a dynamic urban space. It is a playful-looking urban design element with clean simple lines and shapes that reminds us of the old games we used to play.

The bench is made of solid Austrian wood, without any screws and metal elements. The front wheel allows mobility and reduces the effort of transporting it considerably.

KITCHEN BY MIKE ON WHEELS

Studio
Koskela Pty Ltd

Designer
Russel Koskela

Photographer
Koskela Pty Ltd

—

At a time when takeaway food, pop-up diners and temporality are increasingly part of the gastronomic scene, Kitchen by Mike on Wheels takes the idea of mobility and performative kitchens a step further.

This modern-day barrow evokes traditional markets and food transport, and at the same time, operates as the quintessential dining table, kitchen bench or cooking-class counter. With its clever incorporation of a kitchen garden, water, heat and culinary tools, this ingenious piece neatly encapsulates food culture from production to consumption. In its simple linear layout and exposed services, it operates as a wonderfully transparent demonstration of all that is needed to create good food.

The careful choice of raw, precious and technologically advanced materials, associations with place and attention to sustainable processes exemplify the best in contemporary ethical and sophisticated hospitality.

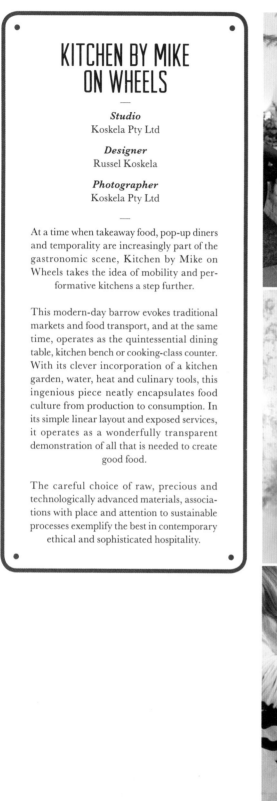

360° KIOSKS

—

Studio
Studio SKLIM

Consultants
WRX Consultants

Photographer
Jeremy San

—

The proposed site for the 360° Kiosks rests on the stretch of land sandwiched between the historical Anderson Bridge and a conservation project, Water Boathouse (a restaurant refurbishment of a former British port office). This pier was the original site of the Singaporean icon, the Merlion, until 2002 when it was relocated to the Merlion Park. This narrow strip of land is approximately 35 metres long and ranges from 7 metres to 13 metres in width. There are at present six tensile membrane canopy structures providing shade at varying heights. Studio SKLIM decided to tackle this challenge and the 360° Kiosks were born.

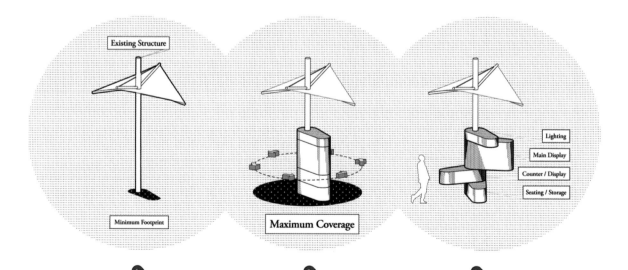

WHEELBENCH

—

Studio
Studio Rogier Martens for Weltevree

Designer
Rogier Martens

Photographer
Weltevree

—

A mobile bench, made of oak wood with a built-in wheelbarrow wheel, this surprising combination of familiar elements strengthens the active outdoor feel of the bench.

Rogier Martens, about the Wheelbench, "Moving a bench with two people has always been a chore… This is a bench you can easily manoeuvre into position. The eye-catching wheel is an invitation to find the best spot. An invitation to be active, to create your world the way you want it, time and time again."

GIFT SHOP AT THE RACES

—

Client	***Interior Designers***
Hong Kong Jockey Club	Hing Chiu, Wendy Lam
Studio	***Graphic Designer***
Marc & Chantal	Sukie Tsang
Creative Director	***Project Managers***
Chantal Rechaussat	Agathe Heidelberg, Selina Mak
Art Director	***Photographer***
Gahyee Tsui	Grischa Rüschendorf
Brand Strategist	
Jessica Collins	

—

The Hong Kong Jockey Club (HKJC), a non-profit organisation providing sporting, betting entertainment and horse racing, is one of the oldest institutions in the city, and one of the largest racing organisations in the world.

On a mission to re-ignite the tradition of attending the races, the HKJC looked to Marc & Chantal to transform their current gift-counter into a retail experience, which echoes the energy and excitement of the races, and ultimately attract the younger generations to continue to attend the races.

An exercise in reinventing tradition, the team at Marc & Chantal used hints of irreverence, and tongue-in-cheek humour, energetic colours and bold contrasts to grab the attention of a younger, hipper demographic, making the Gift Shop at the Races a true reflection of the Hong Kong Jockey Club's ability to move with the times and progression of the City.

SICLI

—

Studio
Bureau A

Designer
Leopold Banchini, Daniel Zamarbide

Photographer
Emmanuelle Bayard

—

SICLI is a workshop directed by BUREAU A (Leopold Banchini and Daniel Zamarbide) with the assistance of Giona Bierens de Haan for the students of the Geneva University of Art and Design (www.head.hesg.ch).

The school was commissioned to rethink the possibilities of creating an exhibition space in a modern landmark building in Geneva. Instead of compromising any space of the listed building with another permanent architectural structure, the workshop concentrated on imagining mobile devices. Inspired by the vernacular and intelligent mobile architectures and spontaneous structures found in many countries in the world, the "on wheels" devices aim to question the white wall and white space as exhibition standards.

The students imagined a series of portable modules that could form a small family of objects hosting different functions accompanying the exhibitions. The five modules as shown in the models are to host: a documentation stand (for brochures and books), an autonomous (photovoltaic) energy module providing the needed lighting and energy for the exhibition, a gathering module including a table and stools, a café, and a media centre with the purpose of visioning film material. After working on the concept and realising models, one of the modules was chosen by the students to build a 1:1 test mock-up.

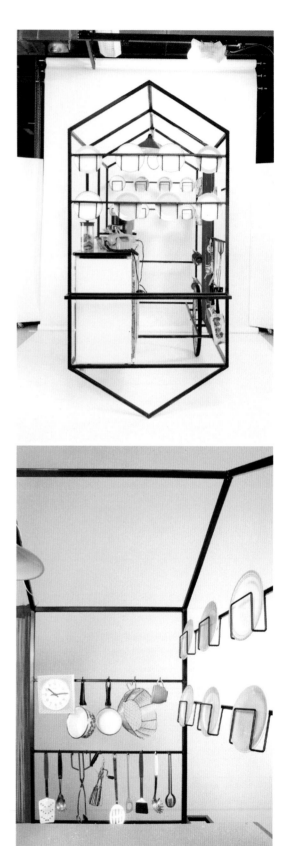

CABIN SEAT

—

Studio
Studio Makkink & Bey

Gallery
Galleria Nilufar

—

The Cabin Seat is a paneled work landscape. An enclosed space for one person offering a possibility to retreat and create some privacy. Spacial functions shift from room to product in this open structure, which is a desk and a work space at the same time. The work questions the distinction between object and the notion of space.

Wooden boards can be easily slotted into the construction. Its easy deconstruction and reconstruction are shown in the construction which is modular, and also references mobility and flexibility. The cabin resembles model making and the colorful, evenly cut multiplex boards give the structure its playful traits. The open and versatile structure has the look of a spacial drawing and leaves enough room to interpret the work. The cabin recalls an actual space from the past; when the studio gathered in a construction workers' trailer to have lunch and discuss projects.

MOBILE HOSPITALITY

—

Designer
chmara.rosinke conceptional design

Photographer
chmara.rosinke

—

The project Mobile Hospitality pays attention to the responsibility and the self-initiative in public spaces. We drove with the wheelbarrow kitchen, the folding table and ten folding stools from place to place to sit and eat in public spaces while spontaneously joining passers-by. At this big table, design meets delight and generates a very good opportunity to get to know each other.

ANDAZ KITCHEN TROLLY

—

Designer
Nina Tolstrup (Studiomama)

Photographer
Studiomama

—

In the spirit of all things festive, Andaz Liverpool Street has commissioned acclaimed designer Nina Tolstrup of Studiomama to create a sensory winter-scape in the main entrance of the Hotel. With curatorial guidance from Libby Sellers, Andaz invited Nina Tolstrup to create a variation on her mobile Outdoor Kitchen which was launched during London Design Festival 2010. Replete with preparation areas, hob and oven, Tolstrup's revised mobile Christmas cart served freshly baked cookies, mince pies and warming drinks throughout the day and filled the Hotel with abundant Christmas aromas and became a spot for guests and visitors to gather and share the festive spirit.

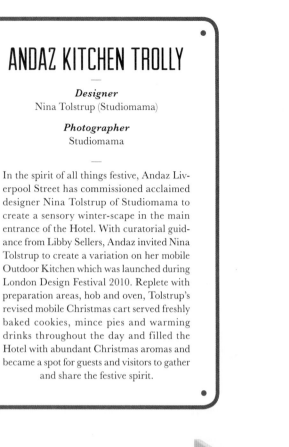

THE LUNGI CARRO

—

Designer
Ciszak Dalmas

Photographer
Ciszak Dalmas

—

Il Carrello can trace its roots back to the Carro Lungi, a prototype display cart for The IOU Project, a producer of ethical clothing. The name Lungi is taken from the rolls of cloth used by The IOU Project to create their clothing. Each product is unique and handmade in Europe using fabrics handwoven in India. When you buy one of the items you'll notice that it has unique ID. Using this IOU Code, you can see and meet the people involved in making your garment—from the fabric itself to the finished piece. The Carro Lungi is included in the limited edition collection produced by La Clinica Design.

KENCHIKUKAGU

—

Designer
Atelier OPA Co.,Ltd

Photographer
Sadamu Saito

—

This is a space-saving furniture from Japan. In 2013, OPA improved the furniture using a type of steel. LED lights and electrical outlets help you use a laptop and other electrical devices. Open it when you need to use it and close it up to tidy things. Wheels allow you to move the furniture to a corner of the room. It is the best solution for compact space.

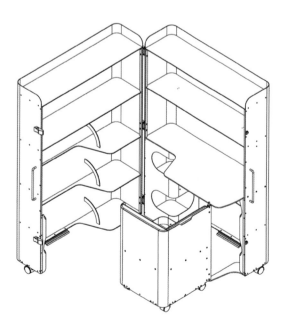

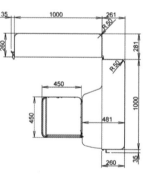

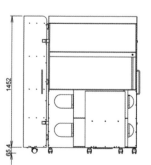

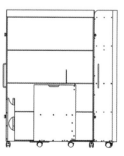

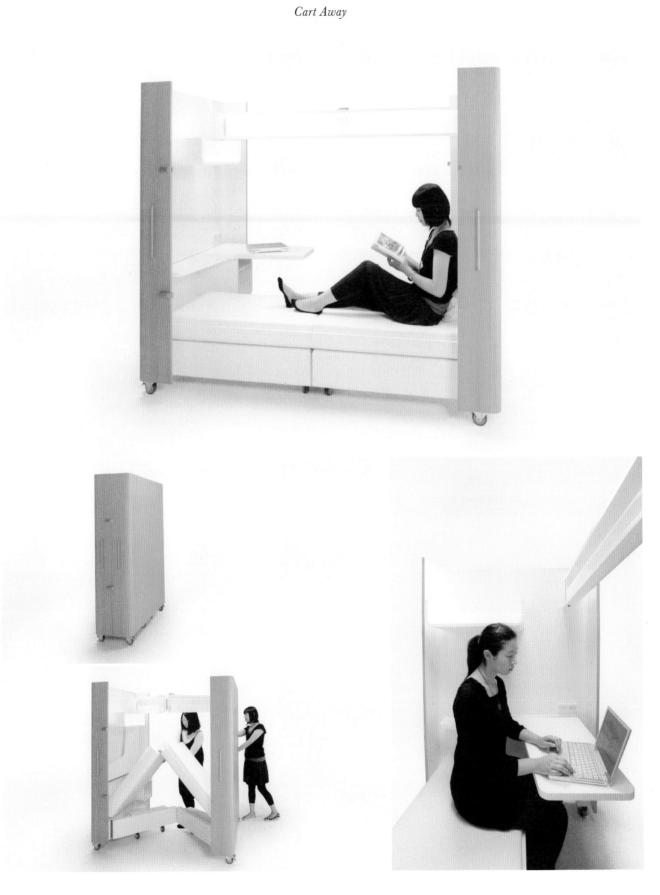

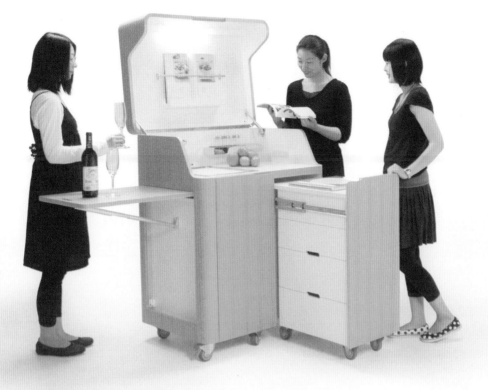

CONCRETE PLANTER

—

Designer
Ben Uyeda

Photographer
Ben Uyeda

—

Ben Uyeda salvaged a beat-up, old kitchen cabinet from a construction site and used it to make this concrete planter on wheels. 2 inch thick XPS rigid foam boards were used to make the inside of the form. Heavy duty metal casters and a chrome spigot make it easy to move and drain, while providing a fun industrial aesthetic. Use it as a mobile herb garden or fill it full of ice and beer for your next party.

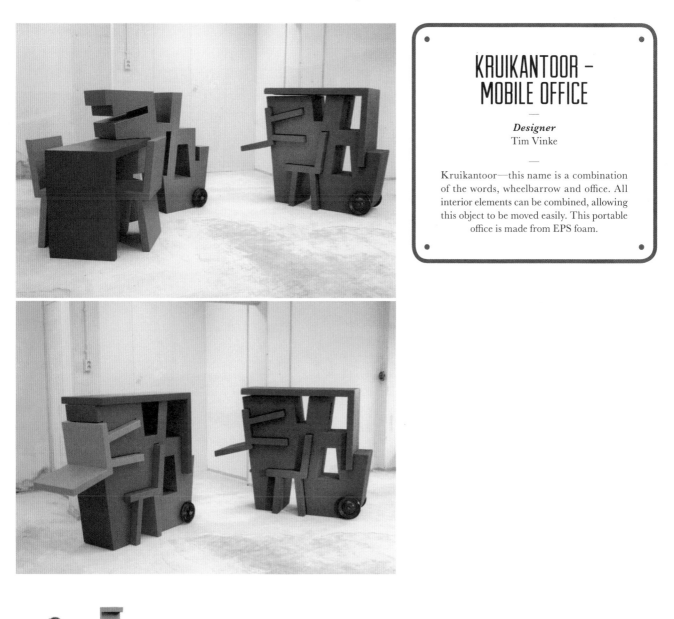

KRUIKANTOOR – MOBILE OFFICE

Designer
Tim Vinke

Kruikantoor—this name is a combination of the words, wheelbarrow and office. All interior elements can be combined, allowing this object to be moved easily. This portable office is made from EPS foam.

HOTELLO

—

Design
Roberto de Luca,
Antonio Scarponi (Conceptual Devices)

Producer
das konzept

Photographer
Monica Tarocco, Tabea Aimee

—

The 20th century left vast abandoned spaces in our cities. Warehouses, factories, military barracks have been built and abandoned in a relatively short period of time. Now, the contemporary city is elaborating new strategies to re-inhabit these empty shells.

Hotello is a 2m × 2m × 2m module, designed for adaptive reuse in this kind of urban environment, one in which interior design is one of the most important tools for the regeneration of urban spaces.

Hotello is the result of the collaboration between the visual artist Roberto De Luca and Antonio Scarponi, and was inspired by the DIY temporary windshields on the beaches of the Nordic Sea. It is a module conceived to extemporarily inhabit the empty lofts of the contemporary city. Hotello is a portable space packed into a trunk. It contains all the necessary elements for a minimal room: a desk, a lamp, a stool, a shelf, a locker. Hotello consists of a metal structure that supports a translucent and a sound absorbent curtain as well as all the furniture needed to work and rest. Hotello can be combined and aggregated in different configurations.

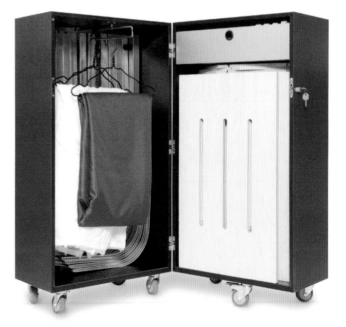

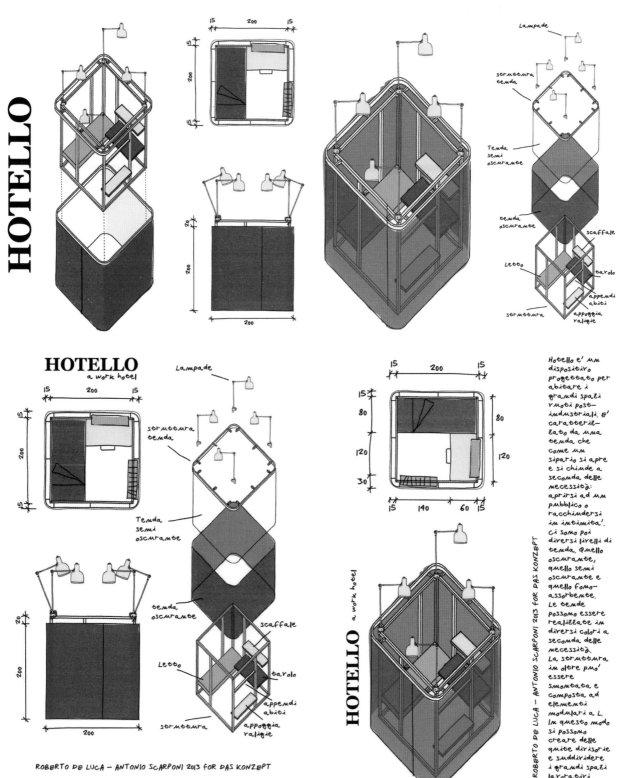

HOTELLO

HOTELLO
a work hotel

Lampade

struttura tenda

Temda semi oscurante

tenda oscurante

scaffale

Letto

tavolo

appemdi abiti

struttura

appoggia valigie

ROBERTO DE LUCA — ANTONIO SCARPONI 2013 FOR DAS KONZEPT

HOTELLO
a work hotel

ROBERTO DE LUCA — ANTONIO SCARPONI 2013 FOR DAS KONZEPT

Hotello e' um dispositivo progettato per abitare i grandi spazi vuoti post-industriali. E' caratterizzato da uma temda che come um sipario si apre e si chiude a seconda delle necessità: aprirsi ad um pubblico o racchiudersi in intimita'. Ci sono poi diversi livelli di temda. Quello oscurante, quello semi oscurante e quello fono-assorbente. Le temde possomo essere realizzate im diversi colori a seconda delle necessità. La struttura im oltre può' essere smontata e composta ad elementi modulari a L. Im questo modo si possomo creare delle quite divisorie e suddividere i grandi spazi lavorativi.

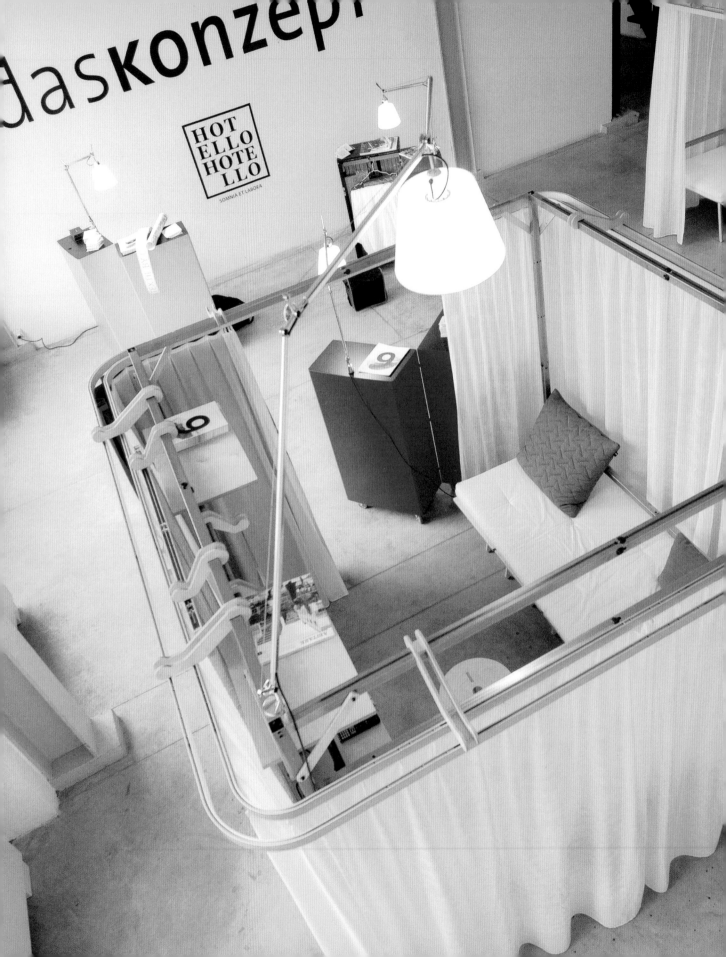

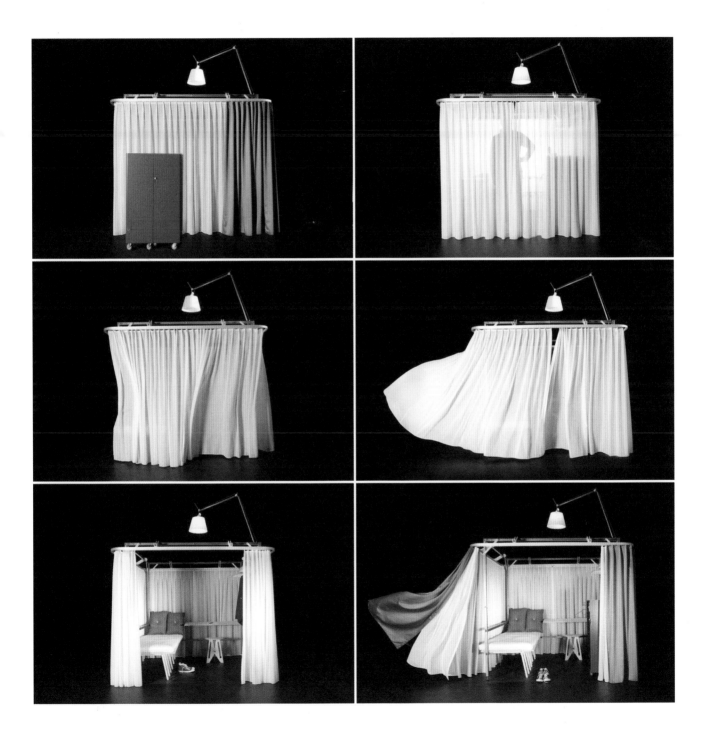

BOOKINIST

—

Designer
Nils Holger Moormann GmbH

Photographer
Jäger & Jäger

Bookinist is a movable chair designed especially for reading.

It is based on the principle of a pushcart and can be rolled to a favourite spot. The inflated tyre provides air suspensioned seating comfort. About 80 paperbacks can be stored in the arms and the backrest of the chair, with a reading lamp and hidden compartments for writing utensils (reading-glass, bookmarks, pencil, eraser, pencil sharpener and a pocketbock). Bookinist invites you to read and think at your leisure.

CHAPTER

02

TWO WHEELERS

TA DI ÔTÔ

Studio
Bureau A

Designer
Leopold Banchini, Daniel Zamarbide

Photographer
Boris Zuliani

—

Everything is dense in Hanoi, including the milk in your coffee. Everything is used in unexpected ways, "things" live different lives, they reincarnate continuously into new functions, passing from one life to another without a moment of respite. In Hanoi, this magic of creativity ends up in everyday life as opposed to art museums.

The blue vertical Bia Hoi for Tadioto accompanies this creative movement. Conceived as a support for small pieces of lives, as an ephemeral house or as a vertical street food restaurant, it might deviate from its original yet wide function and become something else, like an unexpected urban animal. A mini-concert hall? A poetry podium ? It probably just needs to stroll around the busy streets of Hanoi and it'll decide itself which disguise to adopt...

BICI COFFEE

Designer
Jaehun Lee(Bici coffee),
POTATO – Sehoon Lee,
BUMBLEBEE – Jongbum Kim
(no name no shop)

Photographer
Jaehun Lee and many more people

—

Bici Coffee is a Seoul-based pop-up coffee stall. Bici means bicycle in Spanish. We call it a coffee bar that is hanging at the back of bicycle, promising a fresh and exciting coffee experience to those who are "tired" of the city's mundane and often overcrowded cafes. BICI coffee is going anywhere with two bicycle trailers named POTATO and BUMBLEBEE.

WAR GASTRONOMY: RECIPES OF RELOCATION

—

Designer
Chris Treggiari, Justin Hoover

Photographer
Chris Treggiari, Justin Hoover

—

War Gastronomy: Recipes of Relocation is a cultural heritage project disguised as a food cart. Its goal is to create connections through face-to-face interactions, and through sharing stories and recipes to add to an ever-increasing archive of recipes of relocation.

LUMBÜRR CO.

—

Designer
Mark Simmons, Ben Johnston

Photographer
Allan Leonard

—

Lumbürr is a lifestyle brand of handcrafted products built around a day at the park—riding bicycles, playing kubb and lounging on wool blankets.

We strive to create products that promote well-being throughout their life-cycle—from material collection, to manufacturing, to usage and finally to the end-of-life stage. Infused with Canadiana and a hint of Swedishness, Lumbürr products exude craftmanship and quality.

Natural locally-sourced materials were selected to create a product experience that cannot be matched with man-made materials and mass-production. The raw materials, which are contrasted with the occasional red accent, were primarily left unfinished so they would age gracefully and tell a story.

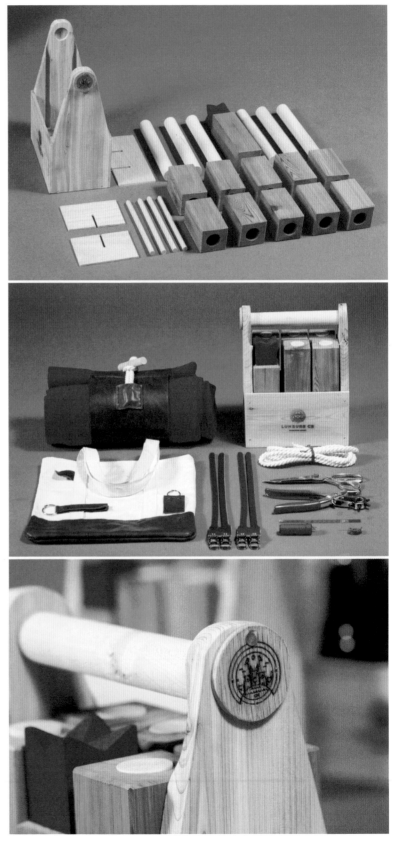

SPRINGTIME

Studio
Bloondesign

Designer
Jeriel Bobbe

Photographer
Jeriel Bobbe

There is nothing like a summer picnic, but sitting down on wet, prickly or sandy grounds might be uncomfortable. This basket offers the perfect solution to that problem. It holds a table for two, chairs and plenty of space to store your food, plates, cups and cutlery. Easy to carry on your bike to any idyllic dinner location, you can have a seat and enjoy a lovely meal in nature. Life is a picnic after all.

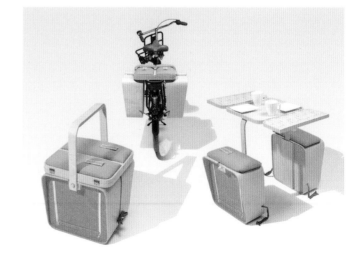

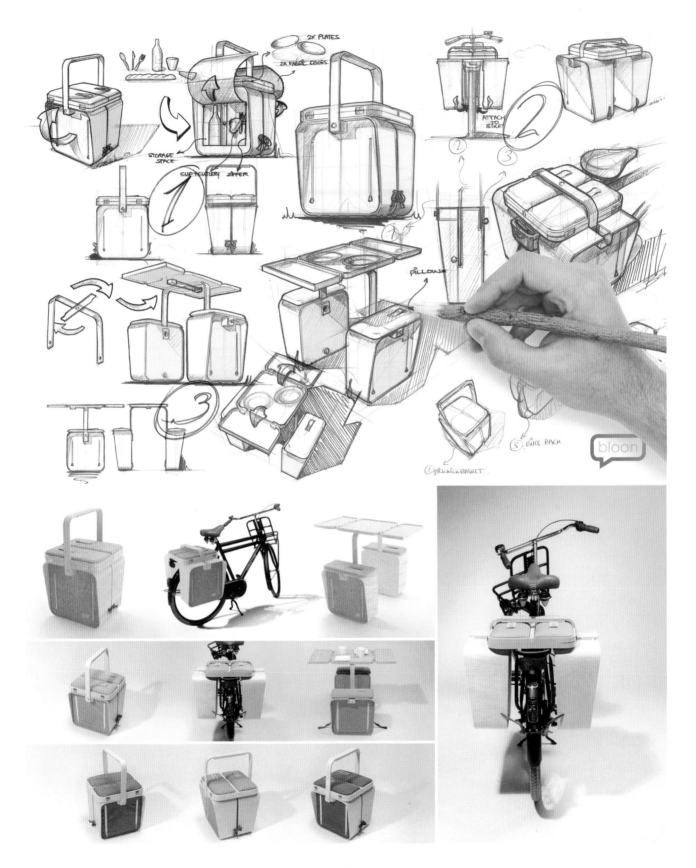

SUPERTRAMP

—

Studio   **Fashion Label**
Lehman B   Rozalb De Mura

Designer   **Photographer**
Jacob Strand   Felicity Crawshaw

—

Supertramp, a communal "Future platform" initiative by do-tank Lehman B (founded by Jacob Strand), officially embarked on it's maiden voyage in and around London's urban amazingness back in June 2010.

In this first project by Lehman B, we attempted to set out to explore the practicality of microsized living and urban downshifting. Inspired by a more minimal, fluid and socially-aware approach to future urban living, the project was seeking to inspire and promote braver and more liveable forms of living.

THE REAL NETWORK

Designer
didelidi, Mira Mira studio

—

Caochangdi's thematic framework delved into the unexplored territory between online and offline realities, with eye-opening results. The brainchild of Italian cultural entreprise Esterni and realised by didelidi together with Mira Mira studio, The Real Network hooked visitors up with tools such as sticky notes and balloons to leave real-life comments and geotags just like in online social networks. A roving photo booth is also present to indulge their desire for capturing moments on the Caochangdi trail.

photobooth

THE TRAVELLING GIN COMPANY

—

Owner
Edward Godden, Joseph Lewis

Photographer
The Travelling Gin Co.

—

A pop-up drinks project created by Edward Godden and Joseph Lewis. The Travelling Gin Co. is a mobile bar serving gin-based cocktails via our workmen bicycle collection. The TGC project was created by Edward Godden & Joseph Lewis in 2012 after a cycling trip from London to Amsterdam.

Our butcher style bicycles have been configured to serve refreshing gin and tonics, along with other gin-based cocktails and soft alternatives via a spirit optic and wicker basket.

ROOM-ROOM

—

Designer
ENCORE HEUREUX + GSTUDIO

Photographer
Sébastien Normand, Richard Kim

—

We intend to extend the notion of natural disaster to what we call "social disaster" to everywhere in the world with homeless people. Many homeless were, are or will be migrants at one point in their life. Our proposal is made for the worldwide homeless people (for climatic, social, political reasons).

Our aims for this shelter are to create a space wich is light to carry, strong and safe, affordable, mobile, ergonomic, thermally efficient and easily transportable. We want to create an emergency architecture to live with flexibility and adaptation in times of social and natural disturbance, as well as permitting many kind of uses.

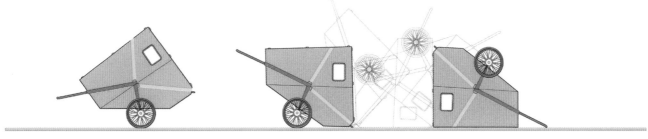

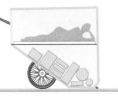

MOVE SLEEP STAY

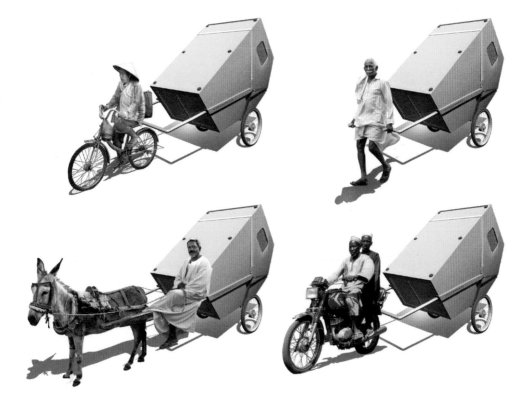

STUSSY ZOOMER

Client
Honda / Stüssy

Designer
Wilson Brothers

Collaboration
Melliard

In 2005, the Honda Zoomer was brought to the UK and 20 people from different walks of life (including designer Ben Wilson) were commissioned to customize one bike each.

A year later Ben was asked to create a very limited edition fleet of 10 Zoomers for Stüssy. Inspired by "classic custom culture" and Stüssy's rich surf heritage, the bikes were fitted with custom-made, intricately laser-etched, wooden panels. (Evoking memories of tattoos and 1950s Hawaiian surf wagons!)

All graphics were designed by Studio Oscar and each bike was hand pin-striped by Melliard. The Stüssy Zoomer was exclusive to the Stüssy Store London, and each individually numbered bike came with its own skateboard and a custom Stüssy Alpha MA-1 jacket.

N55 ROCKET SYSTEM

Designer
N55

Photographer
N55

The N55 ROCKET SYSTEM enables people to communicate their protest in a concrete way. It is a low tech, low cost, highly efficient hybrid rocket propulsion system, fueled by a mixture of polyethylene and laughing gas ($N2O$).

The N55 ROCKET SYSTEM makes it possible to distribute various things from high altitudes. For example, printed matter or plant seeds could be spread over a vast area. The rocket PROTEST, constructed to protest against large concentrations of power, can carry a payload of 2 kg to an altitude of approximately 5200 metres if launched from an angle of 85 degrees. The fuel will burn for 6 seconds, bringing the rocket to a maximum speed of 475 m/s. The N55 ROCKET SYSTEM has been equipped with a parachute and can be reused when a mission is completed. The ROCKET SYSTEM is part of the N55 SPACE PROGRAMME, which aims at creating space for people and making space technology accessible and useful in everyday life situations.

PEDAL-POWERED POPEMOBILE

Designer
Yannick Read

Photographer
Lucy Hutchinson

It's standard practice for Popes to ride in gas-guzzling SUVs. To be environmentally friendly, the carbon-neutral, pedal-powered Popemobile was commissioned by the Environmental Transport Association.

PIT IN

Studio
STORE MUU design studio

Photographer
Daisuke Ito

—

"PIT IN" is a table for a bicycle, whose saddle also functions as a chair for the table. Sitting on the saddle of bicycle, you can take a coffee break, check e-mails using your laptop and so on. Even if you don't ride a bicycle, "PIT IN" will be a open table for standing people.

Wherever "PIT IN" appears, the place will show the characteristics as a public space. Also, this table will open up a new lifestyle of bicycles and cyclists alike.

PEDAL & POP

Studio	**Sundays Designer**
Tofu Design Pte Ltd	Larr Lamy

Creative Director	**Architect / Production Consultant**
Michelle Au	Daniel Fung

Art Director
Alex Lim

The Sundays' "Pedal & Pop" was a pop-up retail installation that debuted within the multi-label lifestyle store "A Curious Teepee" at *SCAPE in Singapore.

Local menswear label Sundays required a pop-up concept for its collection at A Curious Teepee. Something that was functional as a retail showcase, yet carried through Sundays creative vision of craft and aesthetic.

BICYCLE SAUNA KOLONOK

—

Designer
H3T architekti

Photographer
H3T architekti

—

In Prague, cycling is a dedicated hobby and hobbists have to prove constantly that they are spirited enough to adopt this non-standard way of transportation around the city. For those who are not afraid of cycling, we have created a sauna that can be attached to a bike and pulled to a river or lake.

The mobile sauna is structurally designed with functional materials and can accommodate up to six people. However, with due respect to the comfort, the dimensions are minimal. The materials used are light and durable, and the front tilt is in a way reference to the legendary Velorex three-wheeler.

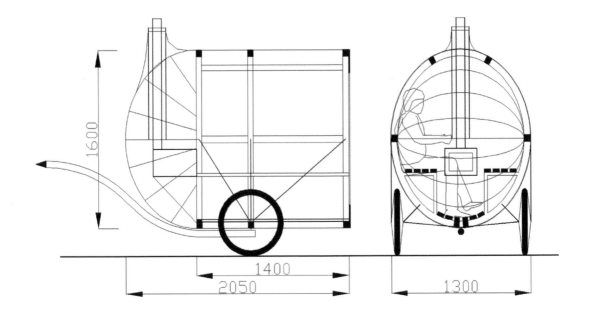

SAWYER & SCALE 1:1

Designer
Jurgen Kuipers

Photographer
Rene Fokkink

Sawyer is a beachcruiser with a custom-made birch plywood frame. It's constructed out of plywood panels. Sawyer is a uniquely designed bike with an elegant look and a comfortable ride.

As a side (art) project there is a Scale 1:1 model kit of the Sawyer bike. Except for the wooden frame parts, the rest of this building kit is not meant to be turned into a real bike and will remain in this form, even though it looks like all the parts can be cut or sawed out and assembled. This building kit shows the beauty of the unassembled model kit frames.

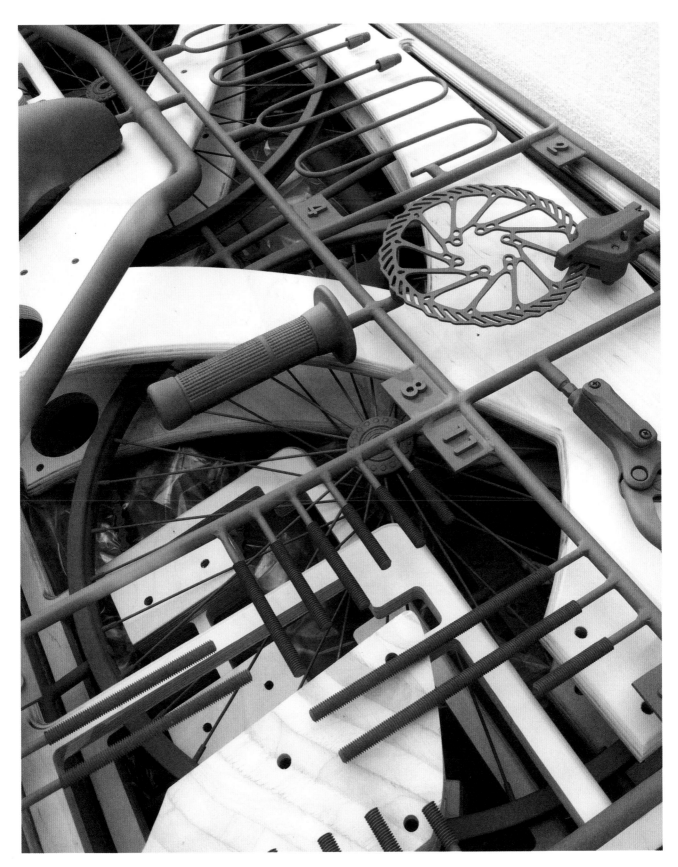

IMENNO-LAVKA

—

Designer
Yaroslav Misonzhnikov

Art Direction
Evgeniy Sadovnikov

Photographer
Ksenya Malgina

—

"Imenno-lavka" (imenno-lavka.ru) — is a new mobile bicycle-operated information center and store that has appeared on the streets of Saint Petersburg. With its help, tourists can receive information about the city and its sights, get the city map free of charge and also buy umbrellas and the designer's souvenirs.

Moreover, on the specially designed counter, tourists will find the production of the "Imenno-design" Petersburg brand (imenno-design. ru). The information about the current location of the "Imenno-lavka" store is published in its Twitter and Instagram accounts.

"The idea to create a bicycle-operated store came to my mind some monthes ago at the time of the master class of the famous German designer Werner Aisslinger. Of course, such things as trishaws, specially designed bikes for transport of goods and many others were invented long time ago, but all of them are technologically complicated and not highly maneuverable. On the other hand, 'Imenno-lavka' is easily fixed and doesn't need a complex fastening. It is handmade of natural wood," says the designer Yaroslav Misonzhnikov.

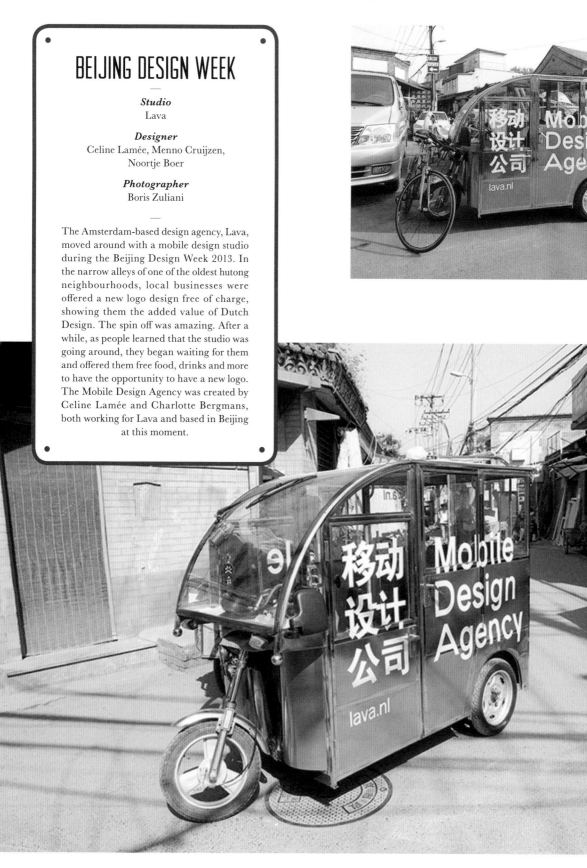

BEIJING DESIGN WEEK

—

Studio
Lava

Designer
Celine Lamée, Menno Cruijzen,
Noortje Boer

Photographer
Boris Zuliani

—

The Amsterdam-based design agency, Lava, moved around with a mobile design studio during the Beijing Design Week 2013. In the narrow alleys of one of the oldest hutong neighbourhoods, local businesses were offered a new logo design free of charge, showing them the added value of Dutch Design. The spin off was amazing. After a while, as people learned that the studio was going around, they began waiting for them and offered them free food, drinks and more to have the opportunity to have a new logo. The Mobile Design Agency was created by Celine Lamée and Charlotte Bergmans, both working for Lava and based in Beijing at this moment.

KIOSK

Studio
Unfold

Photographer
Kristof Vrancken, Unfold

KIOSK is a project that explores a near future scenario in which digital fabricators are so ubiquitous that we see them appear on street corners, just like fast food today is sold in NY-style mobile food stalls. A place where you can quickly get a custom made fix for your broken shoe, materialise an illegal download of Starck's Juicy Salif orange squeezer that you modified for better performance or quickly print out a present for your sister's birthday.

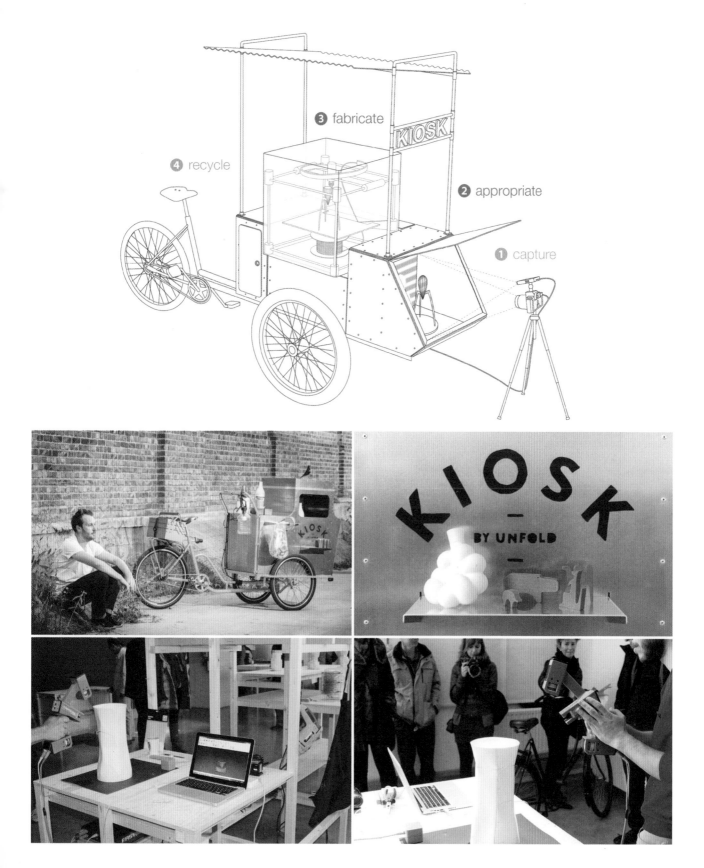

CAN CITY

—

Studio
Studio Swine

—

Studio Swine has created "Can City," a project based in São Paulo where a mobile foundry operates around the city's streets. The foundry smelts aluminum cans using waste vegetable oil collected from local cafes as fuel. The moulds and the finished pieces are all made on location, turning the street into an improvised manufacturing line.

In a city with some 20 million residents the waste is on a massive scale. However, over 80% of the recycling is collected by an informal system of independent waste collectors known as Catadores who pull their handmade carts around the streets. "Can City" creates a system where their livelihoods can extend beyond rubbish collection. The Catadores mine the streets for materials for the furnace, after which, cheap and adaptable sand moulds are made using readily available construction sand from local building sites.

Where the majority of carbon cost is in the transportation of goods rather than their production, "Can City" explores the possibility of industry returning to our cities, using free metal and free fuel to produce an endless range of individually crafted aluminum items adaptable to customisations and able to "cast on demand".

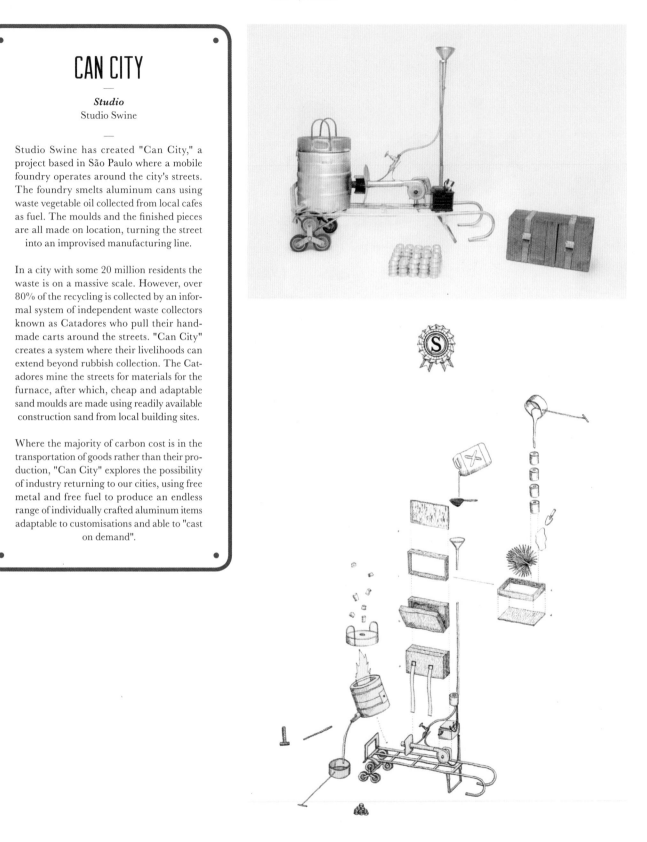

THE HORNSTER

—

Designer
Yannick Read

—

City cyclists who battle to get themselves noticed on the roads can now buy the ultimate deterrent against inattentive truck drivers—a bicycle equipped with a horn that is louder than Concorde. At close quarters the Hornster bicycle emits 178 decibels, a level of sound so powerful that if used in anger it could deafen any motorist who veered too close. The Hornster bicycle was developed to highlight the dangers that cyclists face on city roads, where trucks are involved in over half of cyclist fatalities that occur in London. The triple air horn fitted to the bicycle is an Airchime KH3A from an American locomotive, which has been adapted to run off a scuba diving cylinder.

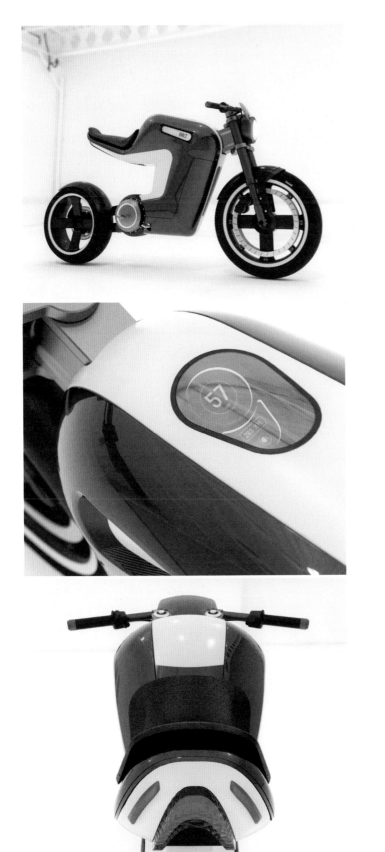

BOLT ELECTRIC MOTORCYCLE

—

Studio
Springtime Industrial Design

Designer
Niels Caris

—

Concept for an electric motorcycle, exploring the design space created by the new technological setup. Creating an electric bike allows you to reconsider the order and proportions of volumes in the product. The absence of a fuel tank and combustion engine pave the way for a new visual archetype (an electric motor and battery as a replacement). The challenge here is to retain a visual reference to performance bikes.

The BOLT design concept consists of a modular trellis / cast aluminium frame, fibre glass body paneling and features a single-sided rear suspension and upside-down front shocks. Sufficient braking power is obtained by large dual 380 mm discs and radial caliper brakes. The bike is powered by a set of two electric motors positioned as low and centered in the bike as possible, putting out a total of around 80 kW, and above all, an amazing amount of torque, typical for electric propulsion. A heavy duty lithium-polymer battery pack supplies the motors with energy. A clear digital display lodged in the volume where normally the fuel tank would be, informs the rider about basic stats like trip info and battery stamina. An oversized tail light ensures proper visibility.

FOLLOW THE CURRENT...

Studio
Group D Creative

Project Team
Cassie Stronach, Alex Dircks,
Haidee Ireland, Richard Neville

Photographer
Alex Dircks, Cassie Stronach,
Owen Hammond

Collaboration
Destination NSW

—

This interactive, mobile creation is a school of moving light sculptures created by transforming three tricycle taxis into giant glowing anglerfish—a deep sea creature that generates its own luminescence. These luminescent fish beacons weave amongst the crowds, conjuring a fantastical vision of the deep ocean, inviting public curiosity and casting a line between other festival installations and events, luring onlookers as they "swim" by.

The project was originally commissioned by Destination NSW for the Vivid light festival 2012 in Sydney, Australia. It has since traveled to Newcastle & Canberra.

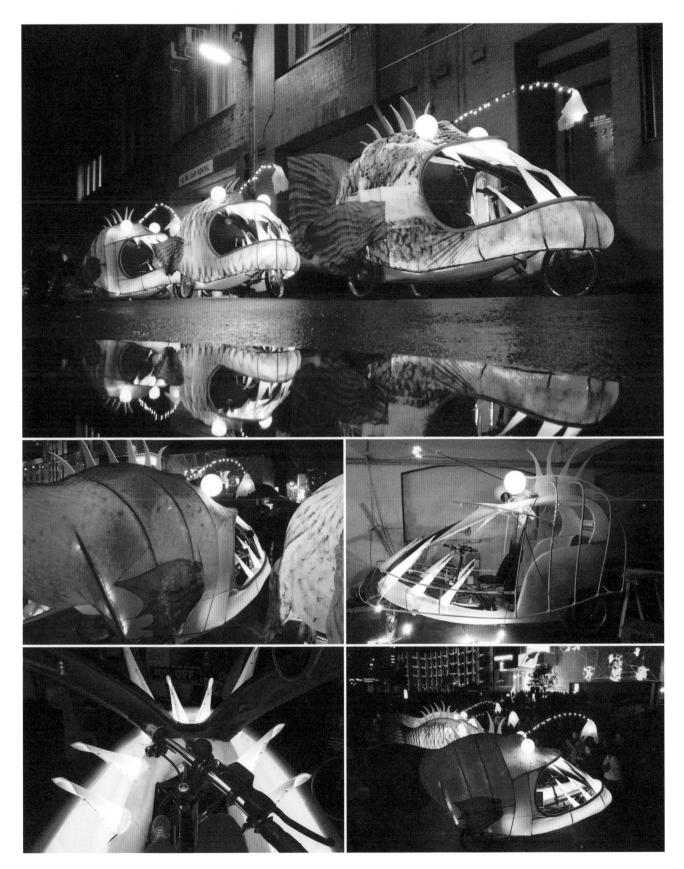

JACK ELECTRIC SCOOTER

Designer
Springtime Industrial Design,
LEEV Mobility

Photographer
Renze Rispens (Springtime)

JACK is a compact and foldable electric-powered scooter. An environmentally friendly and modern personal transporter for traveling short distances in urban areas. It is easy to fold and to bring along, because of its low weight and compact dimensions.

JACK forms an extension of the car, to bridge the "final mile" from parking spot to the final destination. JACK fits nicely into the back of the car and can be charged through the accessory outlet. On public transport, JACK can be folded and unfolded in three simple steps. Given its portability and low weight, you can easily take JACK with you to charge and store indoors. The charger can be plugged into a standard wall socket.

XYZ SPACEFRAME VEHICLES

—

Designer
N55

Photographer
N55

—

XYZ SPACEFRAME VEHICLES enables people to build their own vehicles for transporting people or goods. XYZ SPACEFRAME VEHICLES is based on a low cost, light weight, highly durable construction requiring only simple hand-held, and non-specialized tools to produce. With XYZ SPACEFRAME VEHICLES, N55 offers a new alternative to mass produce traditional cycling products, often made from low grade materials and not made to last or being repaired.

ZINE TRIKE

—

Owner
Microcosm
Publishing

Designer
Haley Tricycles

Painter
Matt Gauck

Photographer
Elly Blue

The Zine Trike is a way for Microcosm Publishing to display our artwork in new and innovative ways.

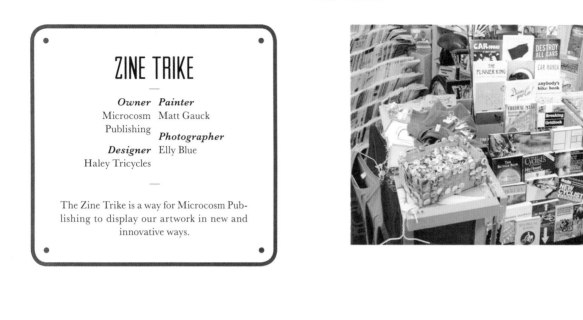

PIG TRUCK

—

Studio
Studio Swine

—

Pig Truck is an urban food stall that serves pig heads in a land oven—an ancient method of cooking used in many native cultures throughout the world. A land oven is simply a pit in the ground used to trap heat for baking, smoking or steaming food. It is commonly used for cooking large quantities of food where no equipment is available. Extremely hot rocks are placed in a hole lined with sand and banana leaves, a prepared pig head is placed inside and covered with more banana leaves to preserve the moisture and protect it from sand.

The stall is designed be self-sustainable, made with very little resources and to function with very little energy. It uses no electricity or plumbing, and the heat for cooking radiates from the rocks which are preheated at the start of the day.

The stall creates an urban island in itself, whilst attracting customers with the simple communal cuisine. The corrugated roof bathes the stall in reflected gold light whilst the split log table can be pulled out of the truck to create more dining space.

MADE IN CHINA

—

Curator
Alexandra Georgescu

Collaboration
Jimi Chen

Architects
SWAG Architects

—

"Made in China" labeled products around the world are often associated with poor manufacturing. However, the everyday lives of the people of China is surrounded by a multitude of timeless, durable & sustainable carefully crafted items. The Made in China exhibition puts on display 24 of these objects during the Beijing Design Week as a reminder that quality, beauty and good design can be found just around the corner.

Each of the 24 items in the collection are floating inside a white plastic box and being treated them as precious design pieces. The boxes are clamped together in order to create a cluster, recalling the Chinese custom of carrying a multitude of things on any means of transportation.

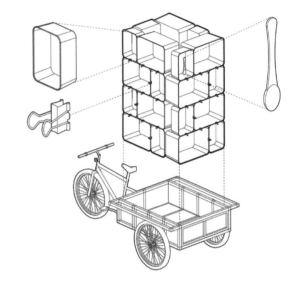

MADE IN CHINA

mobile exhibition of beautiful chinese items

swag

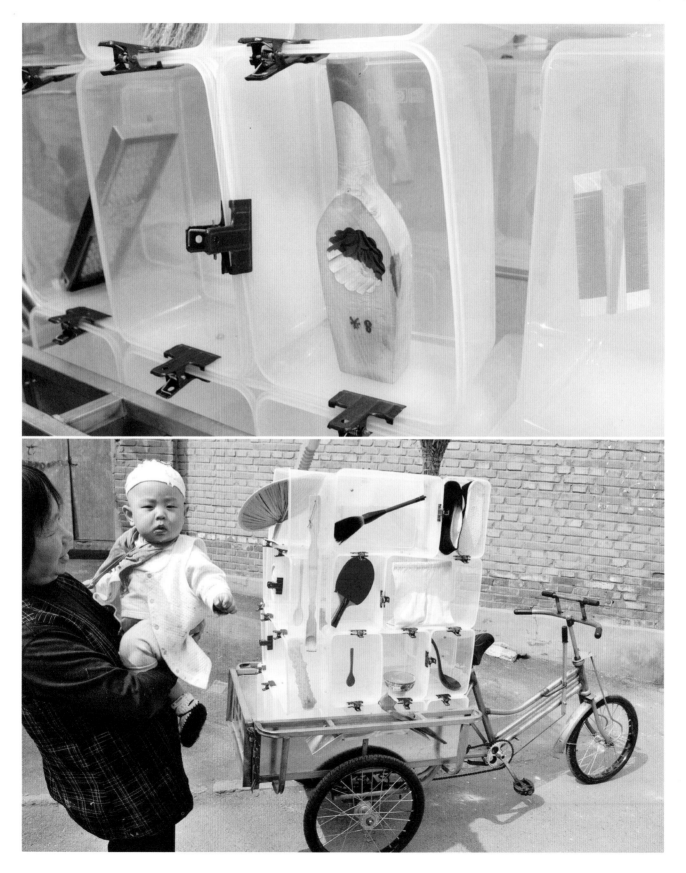

PARAVELO: WORLDS FIRST FLYING BICYCLE

Designer
John Foden, Yannick Read

Photographer
XploreAir

The Paravelo is the world's first flying bicycle—a conventional two-wheeled bike that transforms into an easy-to-operate aircraft capable of altitudes of up to 4,000 feet. As well suited to someone living in London or the Mojave, the paravelo will transform the way we travel for work, leisure and adventure.

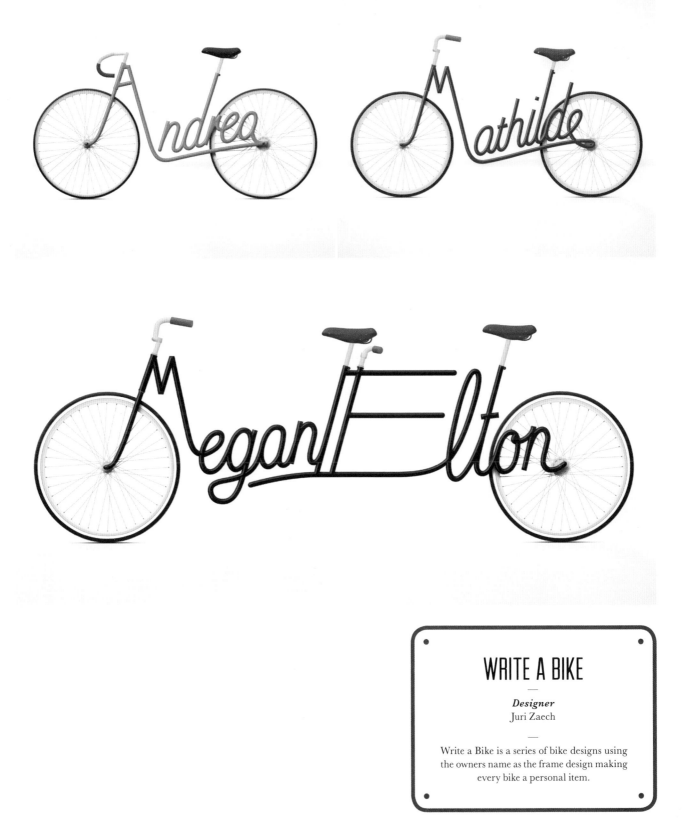

WRITE A BIKE

—

Designer
Juri Zaech

—

Write a Bike is a series of bike designs using
the owners name as the frame design making
every bike a personal item.

POTLATCH!

Studio	**Team**
elii [architecture office]	elii - Ana Herreros, Eva Rubio, Pedro Pablo García
Architects	**Developer**
elii - Uriel Fogué, Eva Gil, Carlos Palacios	Matadero Madrid
	Construction
	Matadero Madrid
	Photographer
	Miguel de Guzmán

Madrid-based Elii Architects have unveiled a rather curious way to kick off the city's yearly art event, El Ranchito. Eight artists will be living in one of the city's most innovative art centers, el Matadero, and participating in a Potlatch, a traditional gift-giving ceremony that dates back to Native American tribes from the Pacific. At the beginning of the event, the artists will be given the basic supplies needed to live in portable, interconnected greenhouses in Matadero's Bay 16. Once the artists receive their transportable structures, which are powered by adult-sized tricycles, they are free to pedal away in the bay until they find just the right spot to set up camp for El Ranchito's duration.

FIREFLY

—

Designer
GeoSpace Studio

—

The FireFly by GeoSpace is an all weather, internally illuminated, human-powered vehicle. The FireFly shell connects to the front of a standard recumbent trike to create a cycling experience that provides a high level of visibility and protection for dark, cold or wet environments.

GeoSpace Studio is interested in imagining the future of low energy vehicles and shelters. Our hope is to create actual objects that address a reality that does not yet exist, but is likely to come. Through the use and demonstration of these objects, we hope to present the possibility for our changing future.

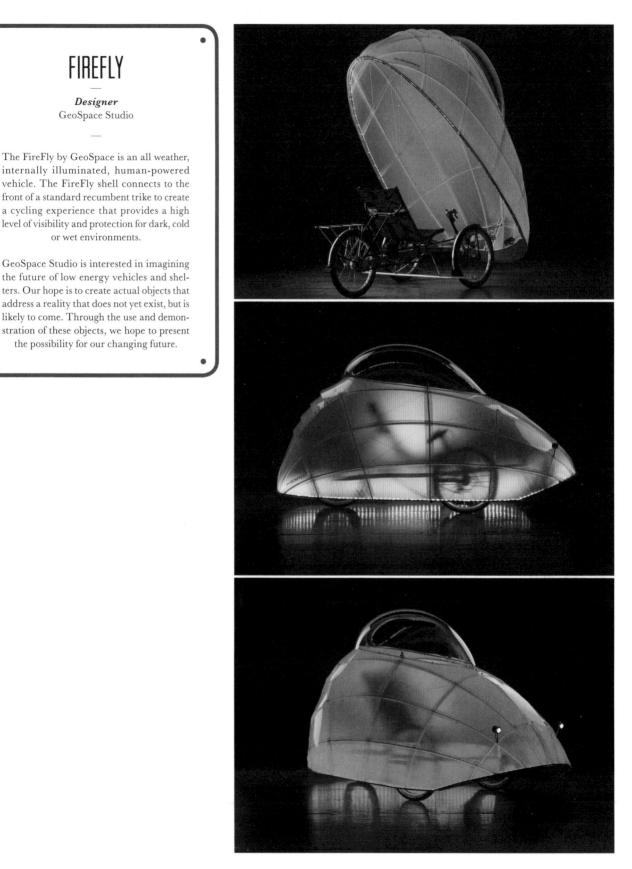

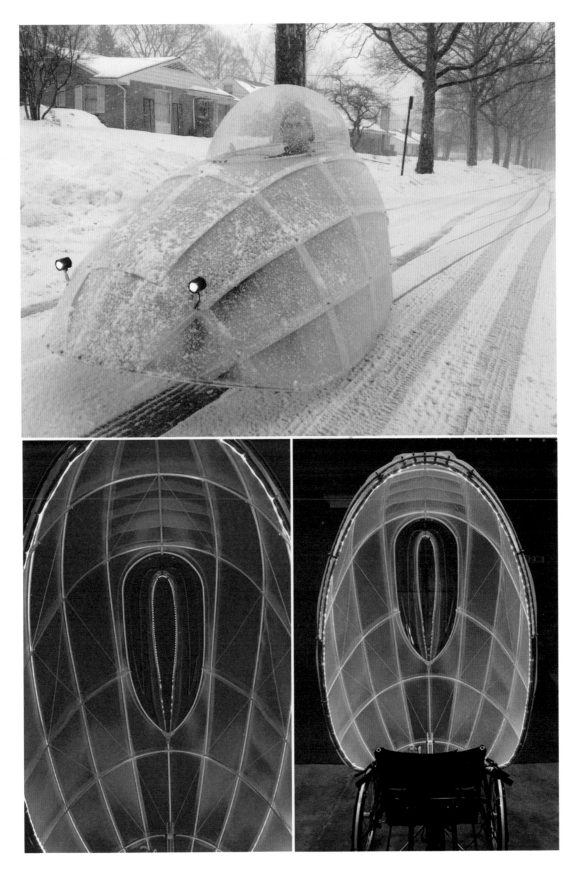

THE OTHER MARKET

—

Designer
Pablo Calderón Salazar

Map Sketching / Toolkit
Anastasia Kubrak

Photographer
Guillaume Neurinaudo,
Silvia Dini Modigliani, Scott Newland,
Deiene García, Pablo Calderón Salazar

—

The Other Market is a platform—materialized in a meshwork of pushcarts and stalls—for trading products and services without the use of money, only using dialogue as a currency. The carts and stalls were made embracing the aesthetics of informality, aiming to create a contrast with an over-planned and over-designed society; this was also the initial trigger for dialogue on the streets. No blueprints, drawings nor measurements were done. There was little intention, if any, of achieving a look to it, but just a honest manifestation of the materials scavenged and the tools and processes that are available.

All of this comes together in interventions, when they stage events that unveil the true aim of the project: to foster public dialogue about relevant issues. The objects, the cart, and the actions serve as a reason and a platform for engaging ordinary people in public dialogue, and amplify their voices through different media. The interventions also play with the ambiguity of the law and informality, for they imply trading things on the street (illegal), yet with no money involved (legal).

MOTOFOCKER CARGO-SCOOTER

Designer
Máté Fock

Photographer
Kolos Somlói

For delivery purposes, a smaller sized vehicle is needed in big cities, especially to fit into narrow streets and to avoid cracked pavements, much like the two-wheeled Bakfiets used in the Netherlands. Bicycles are quiet and environmentally friendly, but they will have problems with heavy loads and uphill slopes.

The scooters of the Vespa have been designed for heavy loads. Also, being a scooter, it helps to beat traffic jams. Using the Vespa scooter, the prototype Máté Fock produced and designed incorporates the advantages of both the Bakfiets and the Vespa—a light urban vehicle and an engine that can handle heavier loads and uphills. Encouraged by successful tests and possible uses, Máté Fock hopes that one day they will develop the use of the urban light goods vehicle.

ROODRUNNER
(ROYAL DUTCH MAIL)

Designer
Springtime Industrial Design

The RoodRunner is a power assisted mail trike for mail delivery in the Netherlands. The advanced RoodRunner helps postmen to deliver more mail with less effort. This new mode of transport enables a larger range of action for the postmen and an increased efficiency of delivery within car quiet areas. The mail is also protected against the weather and theft by its closed and RFID lock-protected plastic container.

MANTYS
[LEEV MOBILITY]

—

Designer
Springtime Industrial Design,
LEEV Mobility

Photographer
Springtime

—

Mantys is a brand new type of electric powered vehicle, delivering a fun and dynamic, yet comfortable ride.

Our first Mantys, Mantys Golf, is fully designed for the golf course. With a range of 27 holes, the Mantys has the power to effortlessly take a 20 percent climb with turf-saving tires and is therefore your perfect companion for a perfect game of golf. Mantys has a unique and fun way of maneuvering it. Rather than using a steering wheel or handlebar, Mantys is controlled by shifting your weight with skiing-like movements, offering the rider a unique riding experience. Mantys Golf also comes with a universal bag mount, a scorecard holder, ball and tee holder and cup holder.

Beside Golf, the Mantys can be put to use in various other applications in places such as warehouses, resorts, terrain inspection, final mile delivery, etc.

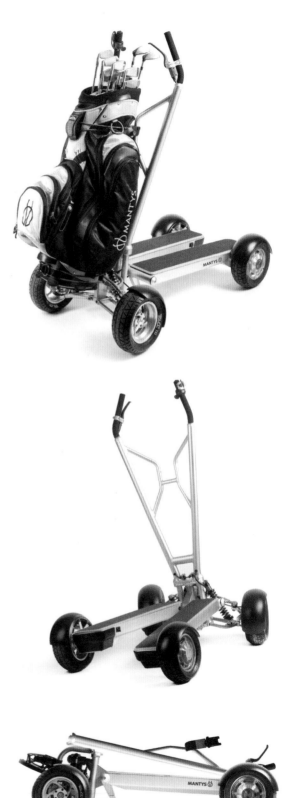

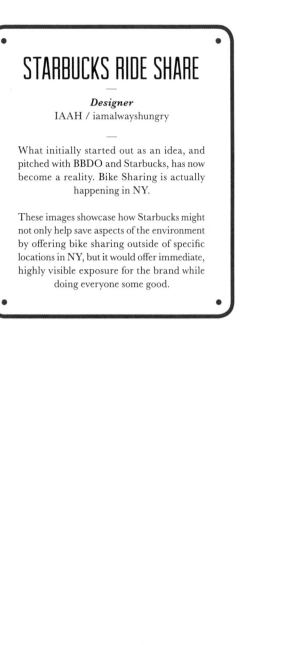

STARBUCKS RIDE SHARE

—

Designer
IAAH / iamalwayshungry

—

What initially started out as an idea, and pitched with **BBDO** and Starbucks, has now become a reality. Bike Sharing is actually happening in NY.

These images showcase how Starbucks might not only help save aspects of the environment by offering bike sharing outside of specific locations in NY, but it would offer immediate, highly visible exposure for the brand while doing everyone some good.

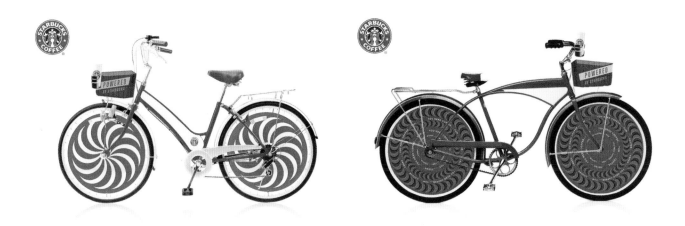

PARKCYCLE SWARM

—

Designer
N55

Photographer
N55

Collaboration
Till Wolfer,
John Bela
(Rebar group)

—

The PARKCYCLE SWARM is a modular system that empowers people to build an instant public park whenever and wherever they want to. The PARKCYCLE SWARM consists of a number of human-powered mobile gardens, and can be combined to form public parks and can consist of any number of individual gardens.

Areas normally used by cars like parking lots or roads in general can be reclaimed and used for non-polluting peaceful social activities instead. Each vehicle has been designed to comply with local bicycle standards. The version showed in this manual fits the EU standards of bicycle design. Adaptations to local regulations in other parts of the world may be necessary and can influence the size of each individual cycle.

The PARKCYCLE SWARM can be seen as a DIY urban planning tool as an alternative to the top down urban planning that dominates most cities in the world. N55 encourage persons to build their own cycles and form PARKCYCLE SWARMS and hereby influence their local urban environments.

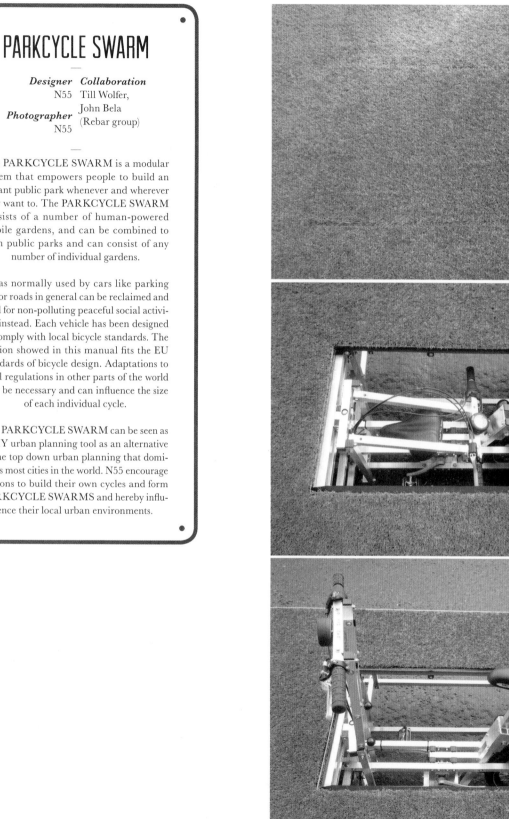

CHAPTER

03

FOUR WHEEL DRIVE

PHOTOMOTO

—

Owner
Austin Havican, Brittany Havican

Photographer
Brittany Havican

—

Photomoto is a restored 1978 Volkswagen Bus converted into a mobile photo booth. It lowers to the ground and opens up for party-goers to take a series of instantly printed photo strips. Compact modern technology in a vintage bus provides the joy and charm of the classic photo booth experience.

BEST MAN MOBILE WEDDING CHAPEL

Owner
The Best Wedding Chapel

—

Honorably named "Best Man," the mobile chapel is recognized as the world's fastest wedding chapel by Guinness World Records. Our 1942 American La France mobile chapel is the result of a $100,000 conversion on the famed TV show Trick My Truck.

It features stained glass windows, an altar, two wooden pews and even an organ.

We can marry you on the road or parked at your chosen location with an unlimited guest list and then deliver you right to the reception! The ideas are limitless!

ELEMMENT

Designer
Marchi Mobile GmbH

Photographer
Marchi Mobile GmbH

The eleMMent series from Marchi Mobile
is a new class within the premium segment
of vehicles, targeted to enthuse lovers of the
extraordinary and visionaries that are sty-
listically at ease. Only the finest companies
and partners have been chosen to contribute
to this masterpiece of German craftsman-
ship. Become part of the exclusive circle of
eleMMent owners. Experience the prestige
and comfort in a royal atmosphere that will
create admiration among others—a feeling
that few dare to explore.

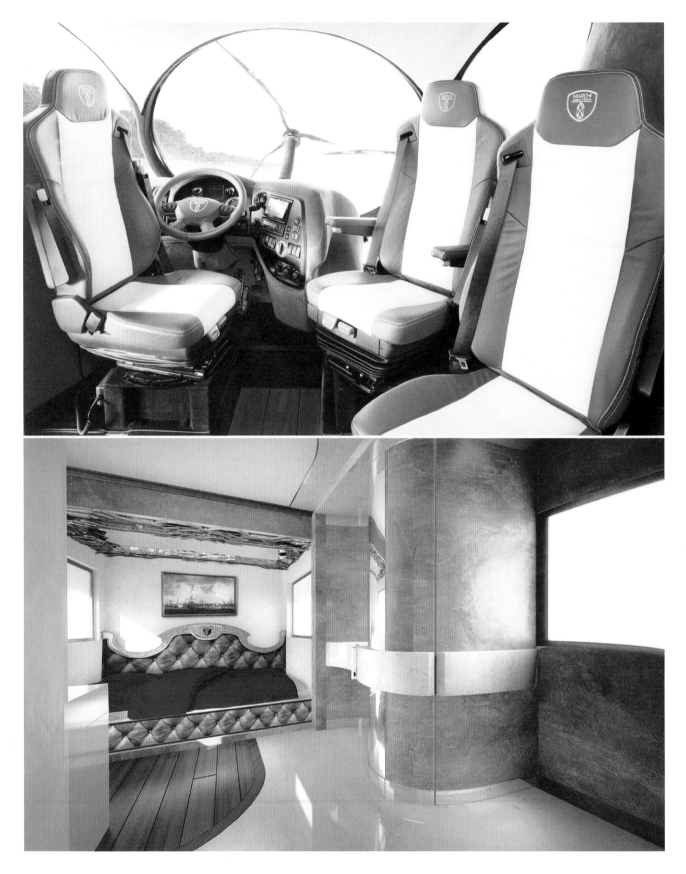

AUTOMOBILE

—

Studio
Studio Job

Designer
Job Smeets, Nynke Tynagel

Photographer
Zero40

—

Studio Job's Land Rover has taken the concept of personalised vehicle styling to brilliantly ghastly levels with a custom Defender project they call Automobile, created to mark the Series models' 65th birthday. Possibly the most outlandish looking pensioner seen in Britain since Vivienne Westwood last popped to the shops for some milk.

Studio Job bridled at the thought of styling a vehicle in the way guest designers usually do it – concept cars with futuristic looks, hi-tech gadgets and almost no basis in the here and now. Instead Job has produced what they term "a sculpture of today", with a couple of wheels in modern Britain and a couple negotiating potholes on an Africa exploration. Festooned with the ceremonial dress of a tribal chieftan, dripping with alternative bling, clownish and utterly impractical, this is a special edition even footballers would think twice about driving around Cheshire. Stained glass windows, a cartwheel, and of course the huge golden rhino phallus on the bonnet all contribute to the tongue-in-cheek fun.

BIKE KAR

—

Studio
Wilson Brothers

T-Shirt
Studio Oscar

Photographer
Oscar Wilson

—

Hand-built by Ben Wilson Design, the Bike-Kar was ridden by the Wilson Brothers as part of the Nike / (Red) Tied-Together relay in London, June 7th 2010.

BROSMIND WAGON

—

Designer
Brosmind

Photographer
Mertixell Arjalaguer

—

Brosmind WAGON is a hilarious car covered with beanbags and powered by pedals. It was created for the collective exhibition ON! Handcrafted Digital Playgrounds, taking place at the Contemporary Arts Center of Cincinnati, Ohio (March–September 2013). All the visitors attending the exhibition are invited to drive it in order to tour the exhibition from a funny point of view.

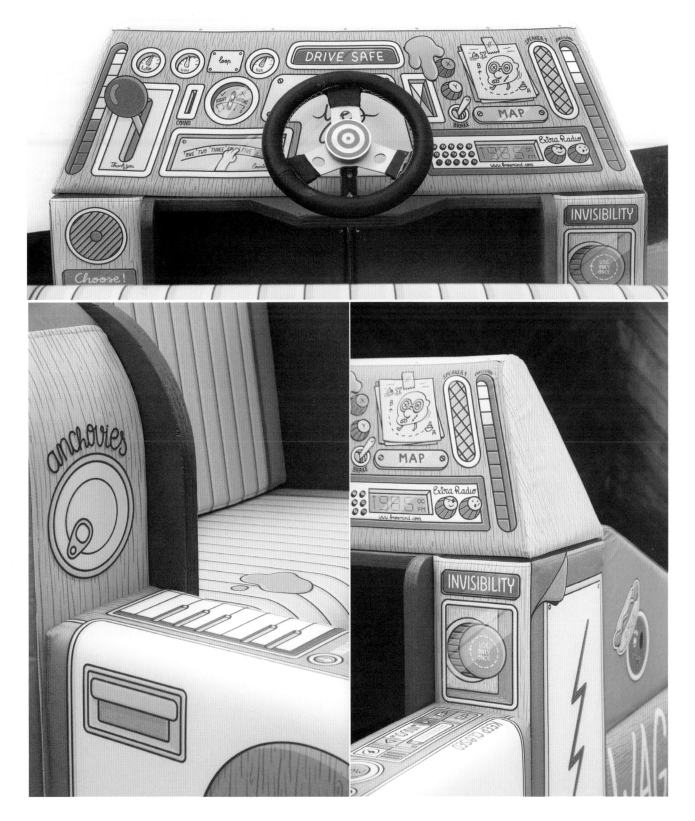

B.O.B.'S LOBSTER

Owner/Managing Director
Rob Dann

Photographer
Kaylie Mountford Photography

B.O.B.'s Lobster is London's newest take on street food. Food is prepared and served up from a fully restored and customised 1957 Volkswagen split screen van. The van was imported from Indiana and customised in the UK. B.O.B.'s Lobster is a delightfully bourgeois dinning experience, brought from the white linen table cloth to the streets. Offering up delicious lobster rolls (fresh lobster filled in a toasted split-top brioche roll), lobster mac 'n' cheese and fresh ahi tuna tacos. B.O.B.'s Lobster challenges convention by making lobster, seafood and good quality wines accessible, affordable and fun.

There is not one single thing about this culinary concept that is not fun. Centre stage is B.O.B.'s nostalgic yet uniquely rebuilt Campervan, retrofitted with a a custom kitchen. Welcoming lobster fanatics, petrol heads and culinary explorers, B.O.B.'s bright lobster-red "splitty" can be found popping up around London.

MY URBAN LIVING ROOM IN BARCELONA

Client	**Photographer**
Daimler AG	Ignacio Navas

Artist	**Coordinator**
Eduardo Cassina,	Zöe Bass (K-MB
Josué Gamonal	Agentur für Marken-
	kommunikation)

"A house is an inhabitable machine," said Le Corbusier. A premise that we have twisted, as our proposal is a machine that becomes an inhabitable space. Our concept is an abstracted blown-up smart fortwo edition BoConcept, a compact car that can fit a whole living room inside, integrating the resulting structure in the fibres of the urban fabric where it sits.

The proposed living room is made up of independent sculptural objects, related and linked together through a network of interconnected pipes, pipes that go beyond the structure to connect with the rest of Barcelona. Pieces are presented individually, yet work as part of a whole: a car door panel that provides shade to a sofa, a chair lit up by a car light, a table whose legs are the departure point of all the structures, a living room that is part of a square. We want to celebrate the design of the elements in this conceptual living room, thus moving away from hierarchies of space, giving all the pieces an even importance.

Wanting to reflect the alternative spirit of the city, we found inspiration in the neighbourhoods surrounding Plaça Catalunya: the graffiti patterns from the nearby Raval, the neon-colours from the ubiquitous signage in the Eixample, the exposed pipes from the buildings in El Born. Therefore, the proposed living room will be use a deliberate industrial language using grey PVC pipes, car parts and furniture. A language that will be contrasted through the use of urban visual cues found in Barcelona—such as neon-coloured joints linking pipes and irregular triangular patterns decorating the furniture— as a form of metropolitan camouflage and integration into the larger city.

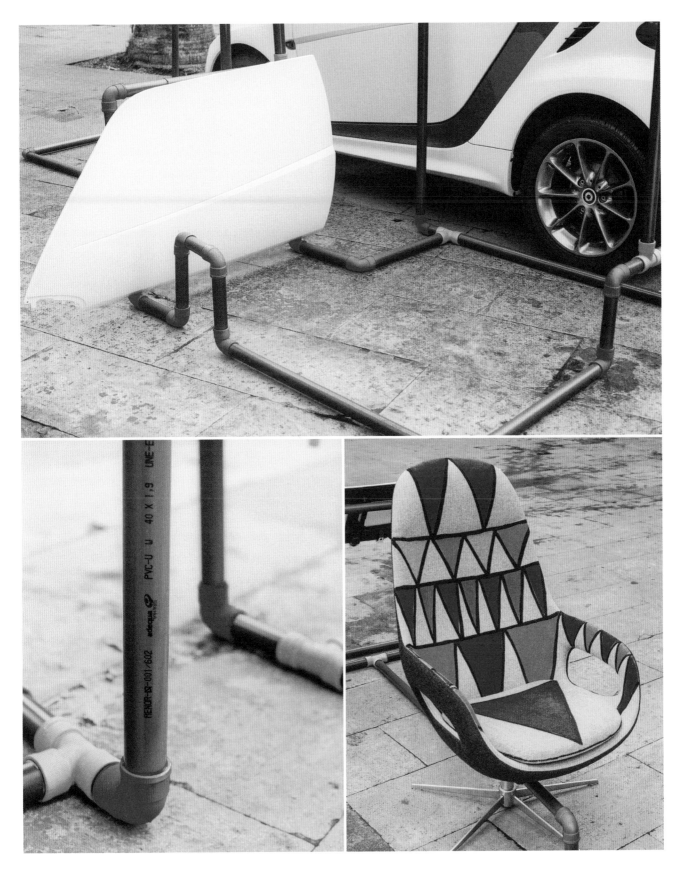

SIP MOBILE LODGE

—

Studio
Von Tundra

Designer
Dan Anderson, Chris Held,
Brian Pietrowski

Photographer
Darryl James

—

Sip Mobile Lodge is a complete tear down and rebuild of a 1969 Dodge Chinook that transformed a road weary beater into an elegant purveyor of fresh juices, smoothies, and late night cocktails.

PER FARE UN ALBERO

—

Designer
Fabio Novembre

Photographer
Giuseppe Modeo

To grow a tree… the very slow growth process of a seed is necessary. While this is an inevitably slow process, we, on the contrary, are able to make things happen really quickly. With help from the Municipality of Milan and with Fiat, we invented a small solution to this city's need for greenery that would make people think and smile. We believe that trees are our real guardian angels—not supernatural beings with wings—but dependable, lifelong companions that produces oxygen.

Spending most of our time in motorcars rather than at home is a result of our restless mobility. Trees and motorcars, increasingly competing with each other for space in our urban landscape, have merged into one single object to become the symbol of a new lifestyle. With this project, Milan and Fiat 500 once again demonstrate their commitment to making our city more liveable.

MY URBAN LIVING ROOM IN COPENHAGEN

—

Client	*Photographer*
Daimler AG	Alastair Philip Wiper

Artist	*Coordinator*
Helle Mardahl	Zöe Bass (K-MB Agentur für Marken-kommunikation)

—

Helle Mardahl created an installation in front of the city's court house. At the heart of the multi-faceted work is the smart fortwo edition BoConcept vehicle, which stands as a collector trolly containing an immense amount of items, such as a skeleton piece from Mardahl's "Ego Queen" pouring out of its windows.

The compact car seems to be teeming with items, and you can open and shut its doors once you feel ready to be immersed in the safe chaos of the "indoors." Elements of the Danish artist's soft sculptural works such as strings of large "plush" beads, and a large cloud of colourful balloons surround the car, extending the installation outwards into the larger expanse of the public space, offering more elements for which the citizens of Copenhagen can engage with in the open living room.

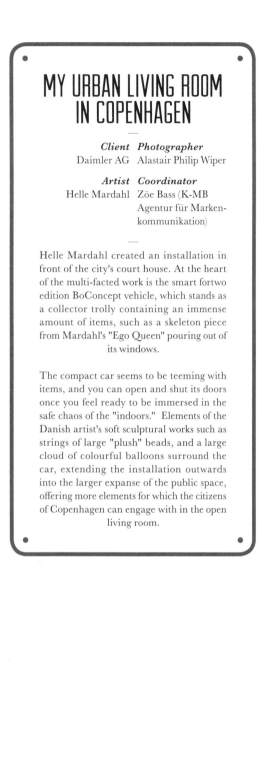

MY URBAN LIVING ROOM IN MUNICH

Client	*Photographer*
Daimler AG	Willem Thomson

Artist	*Coordinator*
Benjamin Röder,	Zöe Bass (K-MB
Steffen Kehrle	Agentur für Marken-kommunikation)

The first installation of the series was held in Odeon Square, Munich where the inner city has been transformed into an outdoor living room. The furniture from the BoConcept smartville collection unites with the smart fortwo edition BoConcept as centerpoints, within which a towering palm tree wrapped in silver tubing tumbles out from the car. Mirrors reflect the public surroundings back into the open-air urban living room, combining personal and public space.

"Within the city, the mirrors resemble pictures, offering completely different perspectives and insights into surrounding space," Steffen Kehrle elaborates. "The sofa shows the car from completely different perspectives and reflects it into all directions." The mirrors serve as walls, yet at the same time they dissolve the boundaries of the urban living room setting to its surrounding, so that the installation seem to disappear into the street. Passengers are invited to interact with the installation and they become part of the project.

"By definition, a living room includes people," Benjamin Röder explains. "It's a place to meet and communicate. This touches on the function of public space itself and promotes the notion of taking the living room idea to the outside world."

TSUBO CAR

Designer
Atelier OPA Co.,Ltd, Toshihiko Suzuki
Laboratory of Kogakuin University

—

"TSUBO CAR" is an electric car, which is the size of 1 *tsubo* or 3.2 square meter—the Japanese minimum scale for housing. It works as a part of a house, and sometimes it become an automatic driving vehicle for transport to a hospital. According to individual needs, a room can be used as a consultation room. We designed the floor level of the car and the house to be of the same heigh, so as to allow easy movement for wheelchairs users. This car charges energy from the solar panels of the connected house.

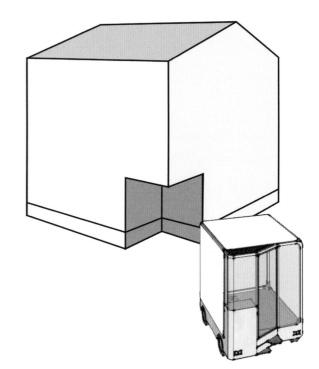

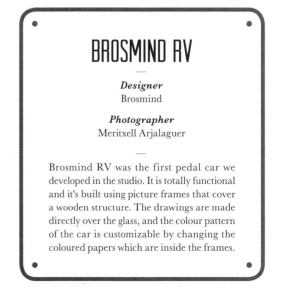

BROSMIND RV

—

Designer
Brosmind

Photographer
Meritxell Arjalaguer

—

Brosmind RV was the first pedal car we developed in the studio. It is totally functional and it's built using picture frames that cover a wooden structure. The drawings are made directly over the glass, and the colour pattern of the car is customizable by changing the coloured papers which are inside the frames.

MY URBAN LIVING ROOM IN PARIS

—

Client
Daimler AG

Photographer
Natalie Weiss

Artist
Jeremy Agnew,
David Myron

Coordinator
Zöe Bass (K-MB
Agentur für Marken-
kommunikation)

—

A hollow "block" of 5000m of hanging yellow ribbons, creates an imaginary force between and amongst the smart fortwo edition BoConcept, chair, table and sofa. The table holds three desk fans, with two stronger floor standing fans pointing down towards the more heavy depth of ribbons at the car and chair. The ribbon that hangs onto the furniture and car is cut and hung from within a centimetre of each piece, giving the feeling that it intersects it.

The ribbon is hung in a diamond formation with a hollow centre. This allows for the public to see through easily through the thin sections, and for more dramatic movement as the moving fans swirl and blow the ribbons outwards through the larger sections. Participants can walk through the ribbons, sit on the chair and sofa, and experience a truly outdoor urban living room, with the wind giving it life.

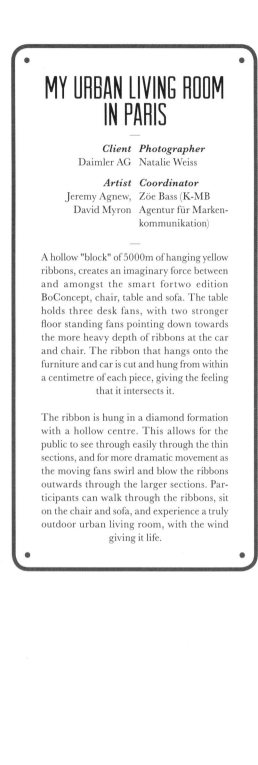

CHAPTER

04

ART ON TRACK

—

Designer
Tristan Hummel

—

Art on Track was an annual mobile art gallery hosted onboard a CTA train—Chicago's commuter rail line—between 2008-2012. Each train car was a site-specific, creative driven, public experience which created a forum for the exchange of ideas and innovative solutions within our community. Every project in Art on Track was curated from local artists who participated for free. Art on Track was opened to the general public who were invited to board the train and engage with the artists and artwork.

NOMAD

—

Studio
Bureau A

Designer
Leopold Banchini, Daniel Zamarbide

Photographer
Thomas Mailaender

—

The installation, NOMAD, chooses to inject "program" into a hyper-architectural environment. This programmatic occupation of the site will last the summer months, taking advantage of the highly frequented garden of the Museum Quai Branly. With informal architecture, assemblage of recycled and transformed objects (caravans, tents, carpets and stools), the installation enables the domestication and the appropriation of a garden originally thought to be admired. Lightweight and mobile, five informal settlements provide spaces for events, refreshments and subsistence. Spread along the paths, in the glades and under the museum ship, they trigger interactions and create a new field of relationships. In the heart of the city, the dense vegetation is the set of a temporary occupation. Without fences nor measurements, this territory is redefined, held and inhabited for a time.

THE GOOD LIFE

—

Designer
Kevin van Braak

Photographer
Kevin van Braak

—

The Good Life started as a collaboration project between Kevin van Braak, Rossella Biscotti and Bart Schoonderbeek. The title is inspired by the homonymous book of the architect Inaki Abalos that invites readers to travel in the imagination, to stimulate the pleasure of thinking, planning and living intensively, and to encourage the invention of a house that doesn't exist yet. The project resulted in a movie and the construction of a house, Kevin van Braak's bus was to be built first as an inspirational model; and has been used after as a platform for concerts, debates, a kitchen and a shop.

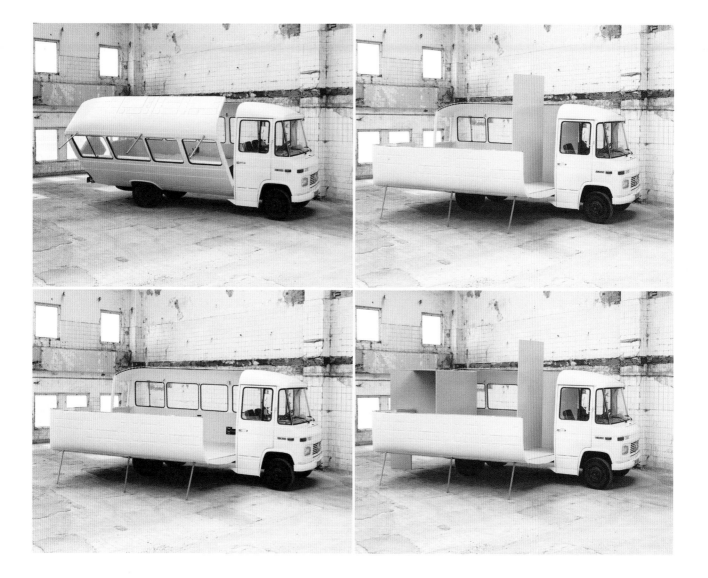

WAGON–JEUX

—

Designer
ENCORE HEUREUX

Photographer
Sébastien Normand,
Cyrus Cornut, Coralie Filippini

—

The site is located on an old factory in Marseille, called La friche la Belle de Mai. The place has been reinvented by artists and the history of the place was used to create a narrative project. The existing rail tracks were the first inspiration to imagine a different playground, and the universe of trains and stations are full of imagination and fascination.

This playground consists of a train car, with three different slides and a structure to go inside that is protected by a white net. We hope that the children will start to dream of themselves, being on a locomotive and going really fast to new and unexplored places of their imagination.

MOSCOW DESIGN MUSEUM

—

Client
Moscow Design Museum

Studio
Lava

Designer
Johan Nijhoff

—

The Moscow Design Museum is unique in several aspects. Firstly, it's the first design museum in Russia. Secondly, instead of a conventional fixed museum, the Moscow Design Museum will be a driving popup museum—a bus. The identity is based on the patterns of Russian crystals, a unique heritance from Russian design history. The geometric figures form the basis for a dynamic identity which will be applied on the exhibition design, the communication, the bus, catalogues and other collaterals. As the museum's "founding" partner, Lava will also give substance to various activities and exhibitions in the near future.

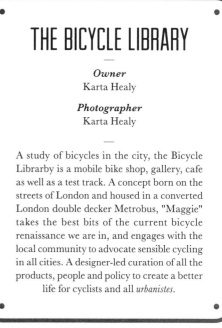

THE BICYCLE LIBRARY

—

Owner
Karta Healy

Photographer
Karta Healy

—

A study of bicycles in the city, the Bicycle Librarby is a mobile bike shop, gallery, cafe as well as a test track. A concept born on the streets of London and housed in a converted London double decker Metrobus, "Maggie" takes the best bits of the current bicycle renaissance we are in, and engages with the local community to advocate sensible cycling in all cities. A designer-led curation of all the products, people and policy to create a better life for cyclists and all *urbanistes*.

HEATHROW EXPRESS: CAKE EXPRESS

—

Client
Heathrow Express

Photographer
Steve Bates Photography

Collaboration
Mischief PR and Miss Cakehead

—

To mark its 5th anniversary, Heathrow Express commissioned an enormous cake at London Paddington Station in the shape of one of its train carriages, which it used as a short public relations campaign.

LOUIS VUITTON:
STAR FERRY

Studio
Marc & Chantal

Designer
Amy Chan

Creative Director
Marc Cansier

Project Manager
Agathe Heidelberg

To celebrate the launch of the Louis Vuitton flagship store on Canton Road in Kowloon, Marc & Chantal worked closely with Louis Vuitton to create an iconic branded look for the historic Star Ferry. The "LV Star Ferry" was wrapped in the iconography of the brand and intermingled with Chinese patterns. The ferry then visually broadcast the brand message back and forth across the world-famous Victoria Harbour.

The brand activation took place during the 110th anniversary of the Star Ferry and linked flagship Louis Vuitton stores on both sides of the harbour. The homage to the history of the ferry was displayed in the visual language of the painted exterior. The French luxury brand's trademark icons were positioned alongside traditional patterns from Hong Kong's past. The colour palette referenced the linked stores, with silver from the Central store and gold from the Kowloon location mixing in the pattern on the ferry.

After 21 days of meticulous painting by a team of 10 craftsmen, the ferry was launched to great fanfare, carrying guests across the harbour for the grand opening of the flagship store on Canton Road. Many passengers had a one-of-a-kind opportunity to cross the harbour and see the skyline from the deck of the Louis Vuitton Star Ferry.

SOUND TAXI –
MAKE THE CITY
SOUND BETTER

Design
AIAIAI (Peter Michael Miller,
Tobias Holz), Yuri Suzuki

Collaboration
Matthew Kneebone, Mark McKeague

Photographer
Alice Maters, Yuri Suzuki,
Matthew Kneebone

"Make The City Sound Better" is the determined name of the campaign for AIAIAIs latest headphone release, the Capital, which we designed for the on-the-go urbanite. We teamed up with London-based sound artist, Yuri Suzuki, in the efforts to engage in an ambitious, design and sound project that literally delivers on the campaign's motivated promise: to make the city sound better.

The Sound Taxi is equipped with a microphone that records the surrounding noises that are part of the everyday din of the city. A specially designed software analyses the frequencies of these noises and uses them to generate unique music in real time. For example, a low rumble starts a bass line or a loud hiss would trigger some hi hats, with the loudness of that noise controlling the loudness of the music. The music generated matches the dynamics of the street, as the sound changes and evolve as you drive through different parts of the city.

Passersby heard the music via the 67 speakers built into the entire car body and the big, shiny Indian horns mounted on top of the taxi's roof. Finally, the passengers of the sound taxi could tune-in to the converted sounds via the headphones installed inside of the vehicle.

KNOWLEDGE TRAIN

—

Designer
Al Borde

Photographer
Cyric Nottelet, Al Borde

—

The train car has been selected to be part of the railway system recovery program by the Ecuadorian Ministry of Culture & Heritage. But unlike other elements that make up this restoration project, this boxcar carries neither freight nor tourists, but culture and public space.

The reactivation of the railway is a great event for the communities along its route. After 12 years of absence, these settlements not only recover a form of communication and reactivated economically, but they also recover, in many cases, their vocations.

Cultural promoters will use the train car as an activator of public spaces in the stations where it stops. The train car is able to host musical performances, theater, community training, celebrations and more. The car does not have a strictly defined architectural program, posing a challenge to the architects to design it to work for any activity that the cultural promoters schedule.

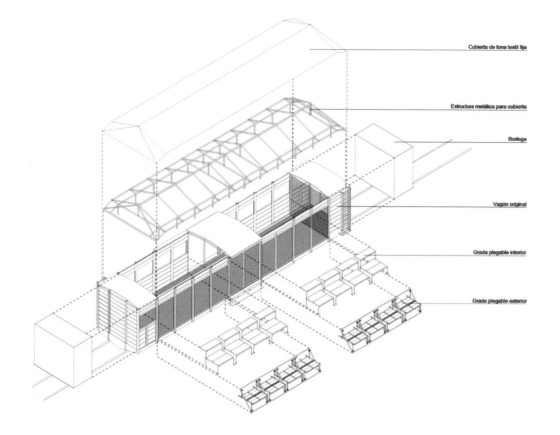

Cubierta de lona textil fija

Estructura metálica para cubierta

Bodega

Vagón original

Grada plegable interior

Grada plegable exterior

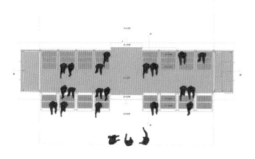

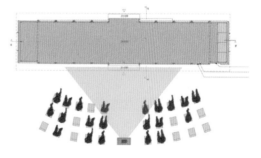

CORTE A-A'

CORTE A-A'

CHAPTER

05

CURRY UP NOW

—

Designer
Design Womb

Photographer
Michelle Edmunds Photography

—

Hungry or not, here it comes. Curry Up Now is known as one of the first food trucks to hit the San Francisco Bay Area culinary scene. They specialize in authentic Indian street food with a fusion twist.

Northern California's edgy street food scene is growing and very popular. The Curry Up Now truck needs to stand out on its own on a crowded street or amongst a small pack of food trucks. The hand-drawn logotype is paired with bold playful patterns and a curry-inspired colour palette. With a menu selling "sexy fries" it was important for the brand to stay true to the food's own personality. It had to make a statement. The result is a truck design that is bright, full of flavour and demands attention.

SOLAR-POWERED POPSICLE TRUCK

—

Art Direction / Truck Buildout
Jason Anello

Graphics / Art Direction
Kelli Anderson

—

This solar powered popsicle truck is rolling around the United States, evangelizing the concept of a solar-powered home and handing out free, artisanally made popsicles. The multitasking truck actually runs off on solar energy itself, so it is basically a physical infographic on wheels.

As people queue around the truck, they are brought into close range of the infographics. The statistics are incredible and they quickly reveal that the amount of energy needed to fuel all human activity is trivial when compared to the amount of energy in a day's worth of sunlight. And yet, solar accounts for less than 1% of all energy in the United States. With any luck, this combination of sugar, facts, and the threat of humanity's self-inflicted demise owing to dirty energy will be persuasive enough to get some people off the grid.

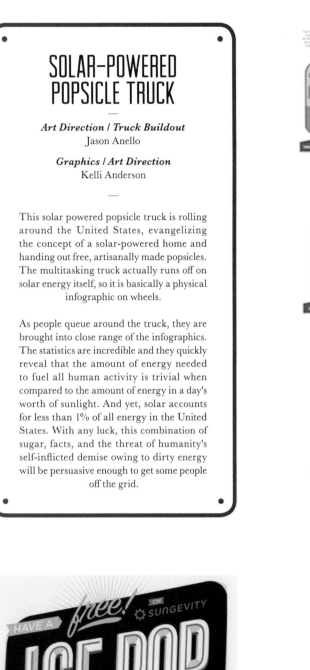

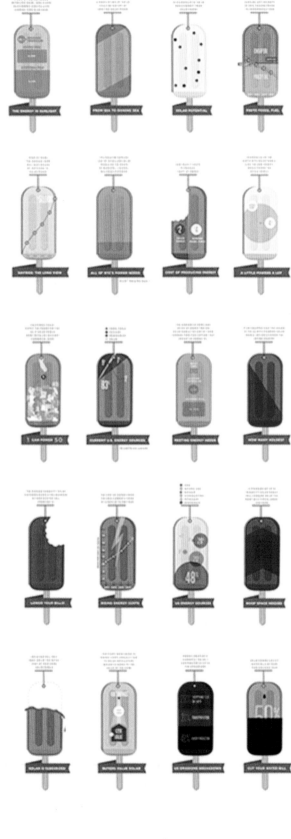

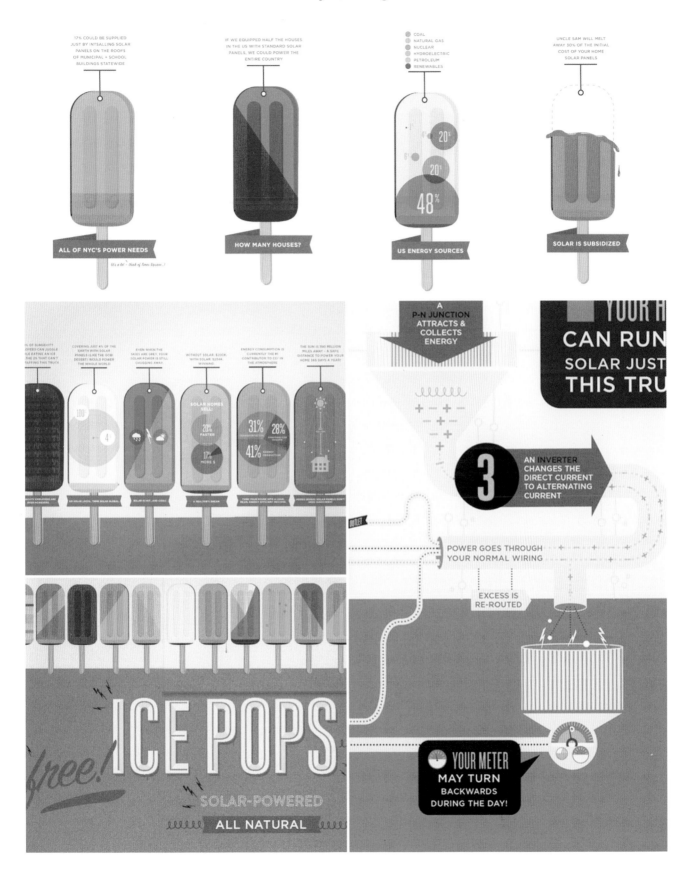

TINY TRAVELLING THEATRE

—

Designer
aberrant architecture

Photographer
aberrant architecture, Simon Kennedy

—

The Tiny Travelling Theatre gave its debut performance at Clerkenwell Design Week 2012. The mobile theatre, which was towed by a camper van, toured Clerkenwell and occupied multiple sites. Inside, an audience of up to six people enjoyed a series of intimate performances, which explored the intense emotion of a micro live performance.

NEBULA

Architects *Engineer*
Andrew Maynard Advanced Design
Innovations
Builder
Michael Whytlaw *Photographers*
Jorge de araujo,
Nic Granleese

Nebula is a revolution in inclusive design. As Australia's first portable arts space created with the needs of artists with a disability at the centre of its design, the Nebula studio adapts to the art and the artists. By placing the needs and intentions of the artists at the centre of its function, Nebula can be transformed into a gallery, workshop / seminar space or performing arts venue. In each capacity, Nebula accommodates any type of creative work produced by artists with a disability, offers opportunities for creating site-specific work, and can be used as a communal meeting place. Through this space, artists with a disability can inject their work into the mainstream arts community.

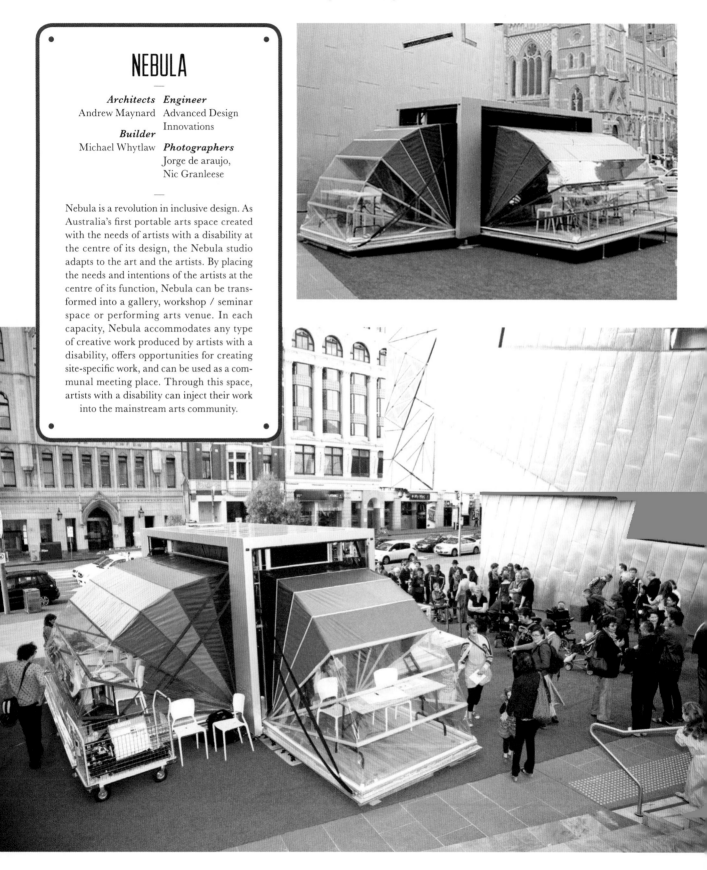

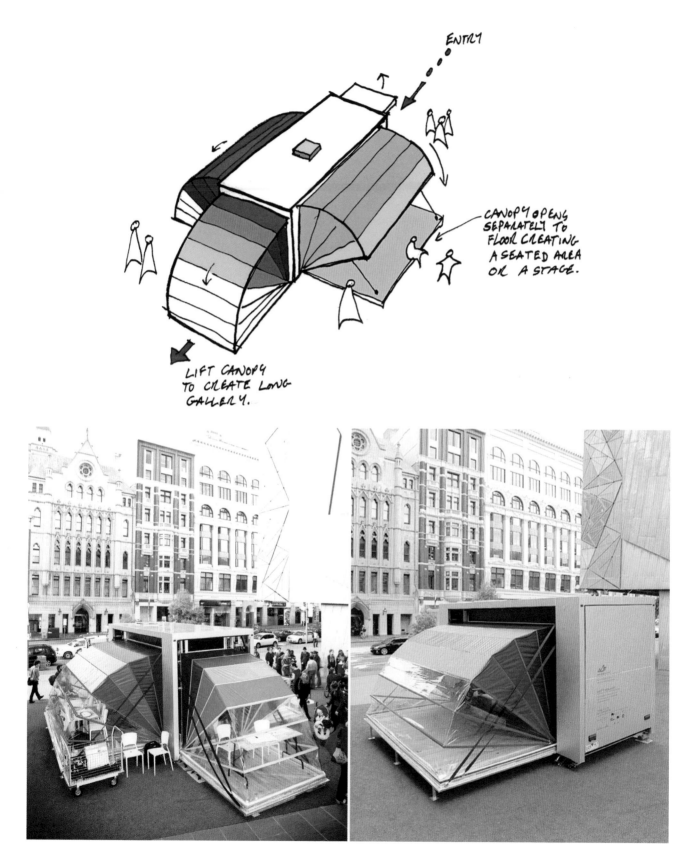

ENTRY

CANOPY OPENS
SEPARATELY TO
FLOOR CREATING
A SEATED AREA
OR A STAGE.

LIFT CANOPY
TO CREATE LONG
GALLERY.

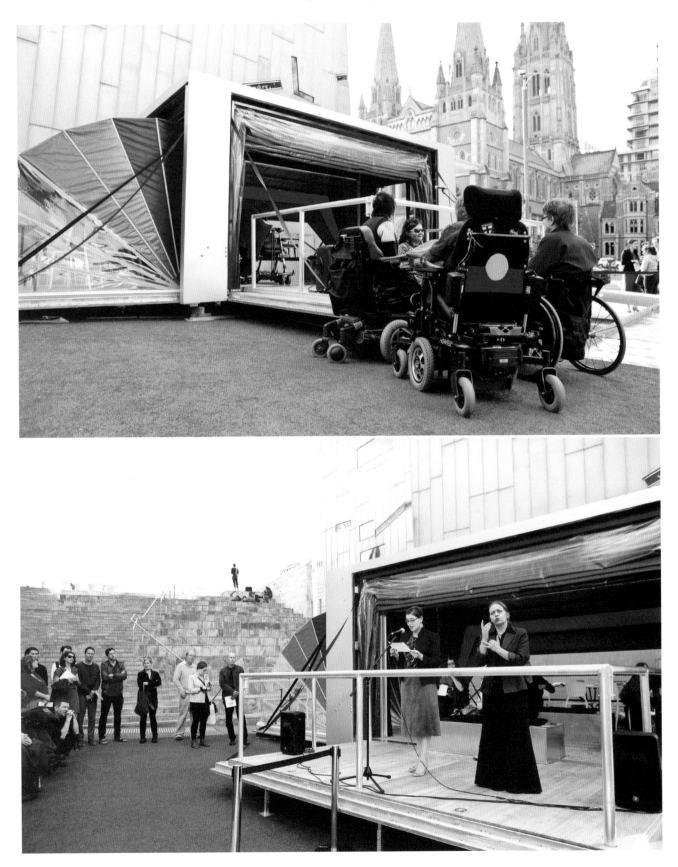

ANDELINA

—

Studio
otto design lab.

Producer
Ken Noguchi

Client
naniwa seian

Photographer
Kazufumi Nakamura

Designer
Takahiro Ichino

Illustrator
Mari Maeda

Creative Director
Yuki Hisada

Public Relations
Aya Takahashi

—

"Wagashi" are traditional Japanese sweets. Some contain "anko," which is a sweet, red-bean paste. In recent years, western sweets have become more popular with young people in Japan. "Andelina Go" is a mobile catering van that provides both delivery and also sells the "anko" sweets at various locations in Osaka. The customer can call via Twitter and have Andelina deliver the sweets. "Andelina" is a total renovation of the image of "anko."

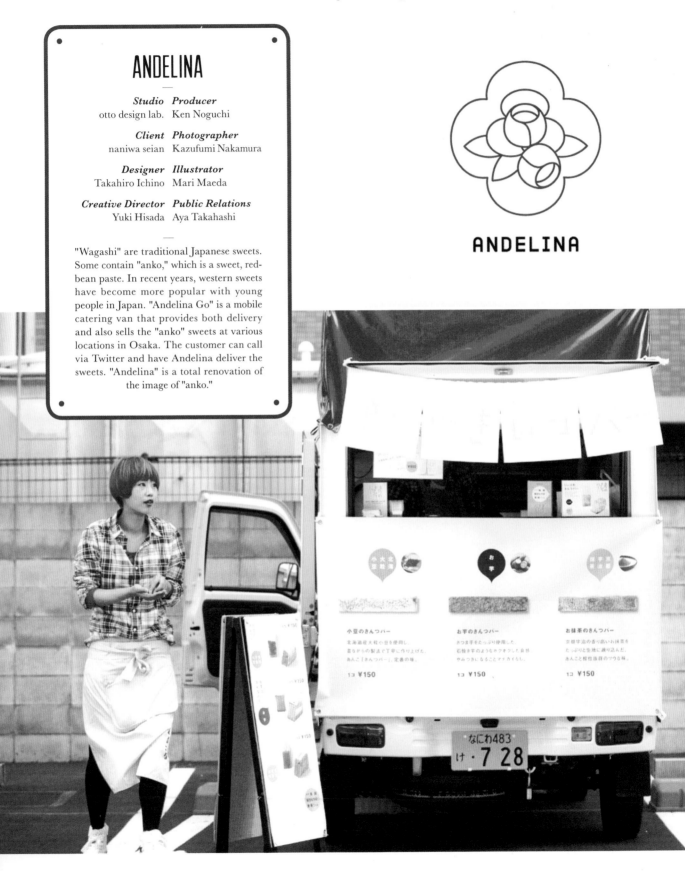

ANDELINA

STREET SURFER

Designer
Design Womb

Photographer
Esther Louise Photography

Street Surfer is a fresh food eatery food truck roaming the streets of Tampa Bay, Florida.

BOT POD

—

Architects
Andrew Maynard

Builder
Astralyte

Construction Manager
Derek Myers

Photographers
Kevin Hui,
Michael Ong

—

The Botanic Gardens approached AMA to create a mobile visitors pod for their "Garden Ambassadors" (volunteers) to use. The pod was to be taken to different parts of the garden that coincides with annual events. For example, the pod can moved to the flowering of specific plants, where ambassadors could share their knowledge and a wealth of history and ecology at the gardens, with the visitors.

The proposed pod was a simple timber cube with a green roof—a large planter box when not in use. The box unfolds to reveal information about the gardens, a space to educate about the potting of differing species of plants as well as a space to explore seed types and discuss the history of the gardens. A bench can be folded down for chats with visitors or a casual cup of tea between ambassadors.

More importantly, the design should avoid a display wall that opens in a single direction to encourage more interaction. The pod folds out to define different spaces while still connected to each other. The visitor can then wander around the pod to discover more information on their own or interact with ambassadors directly.

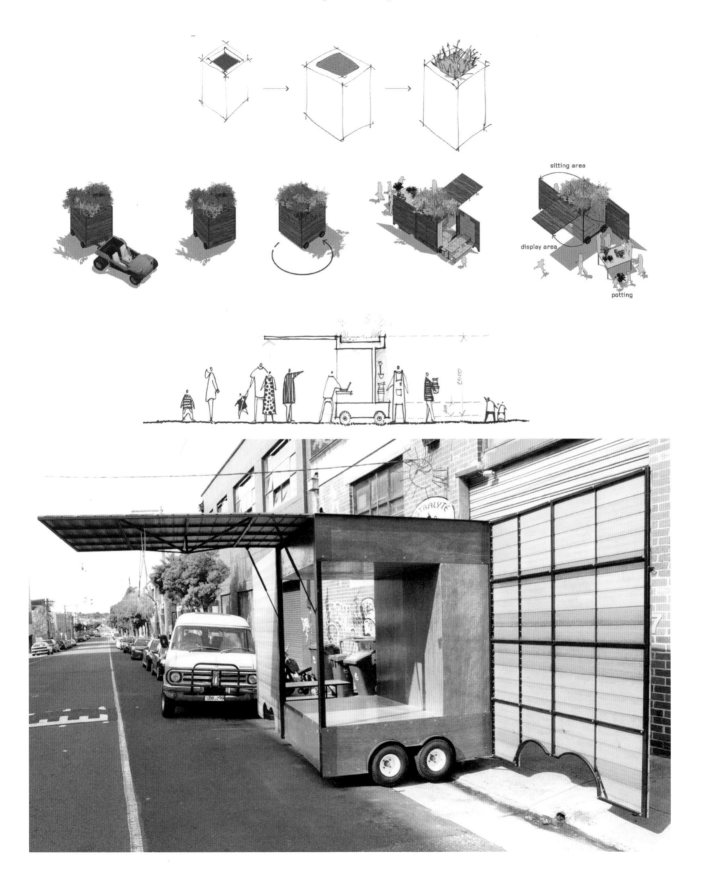

HÜTTENPALAST

—

Designer
Sarah Vollmer

Photographer
Jan Brockhaus

—

Hüttenpalast is a little "indoor camping site" which is located in the heart of Berlin. Set up by former event planner Silke Lorenzen and designer Sarah Vollmer, the Hüttenpalast aims to retain the community-spirited atmosphere of a campsite, despite the fact that the rooms are located in the large, open space of a former vacuum-cleaning factory. For anyone who require more privacy, they can stay in one of the six spacious and modern designed hotel rooms.

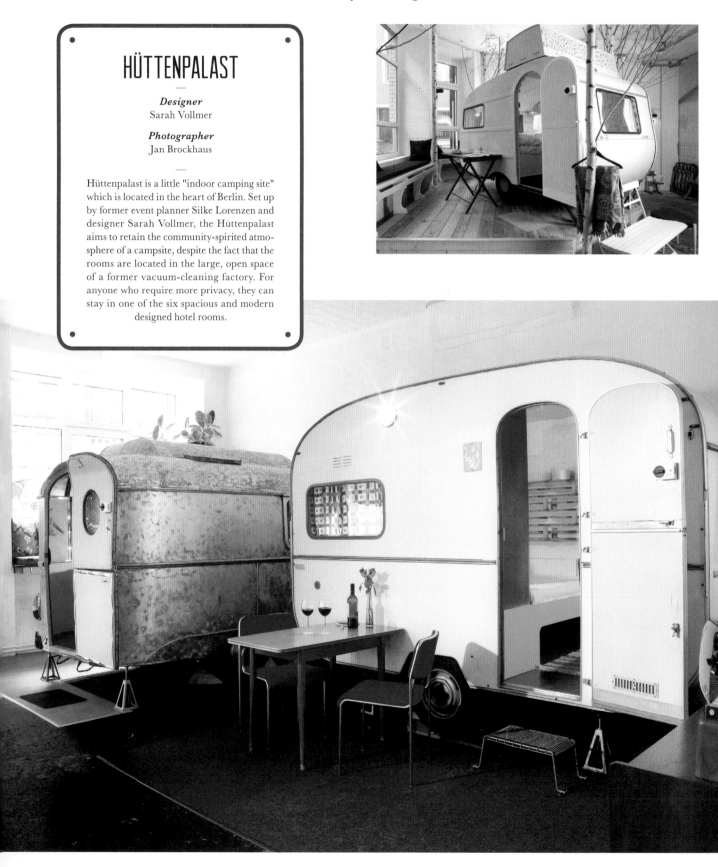

MARKIES

—

Studio
Böhtlingk architectuur

Designer
Eduard Böhtlingk

Photographer
Roos Aldershoff

—

The Markies (Dutch for "awning") is a caravan, or a mobile home, that folds out by a motorized device to triple its floor area at its destination. The side walls descend to create two new zones for living. In one zone is the living room or terrace, where it is covered by a transparent awning and can be left open in fine weather. The other zone is the bedroom, where it is covered by an opaque awning and can be spilt into two parts. The kitchen, dining space and bathroom are situated in the solid central area.

MOBILE ARTS PLATFORM, MAP

Designer
Chris Treggiari, Peter Foucault

Photographer
Chris Treggiari, Peter Foucault

MAP: The Mobile Arts Platform (MAP) is a Bay Area artmaking and curatorial team founded in 2009 by Peter Foucualt and Chris Treggiari, with the goal of creating mobile exhibition structures that engage the public. MAP creates an autonomous exhibition space and an artistic research lab where a cross pollination of mediums and genres can occur, be accessible to the public, and create strong bonds with partner communities.

THE MOBILE EXHIBITION LAB

—

Designer
Gabor Palotai Design

—

The Mobile Exhibition Lab is a mobile technology laboratory that is intended for Swedish museums and their staff. The mobile lab is touring Sweden in 2012 and 2013. At each stop, workshops and lectures will be held on subjects related to exhibitions. By combining the client's existing symbol (the square and the comma) with question marks, exclamation marks and interjections like "hm?!" and "aha!", the whole process of experimenting, learning and understanding could be manifested in a unique graphical language. The choice of contrasting colours achieves a strong signalling effect in the city-scape and while on the road.

ROAMING MARKET

—

Designer
aberrant architecture

Photographer
aberrant architecture, Ben Quinton

—

The "Roaming Market" mobile structure was created for Lower Marsh Market in London Waterloo. The Roaming Market can be moved to different sites, and once situated, the compact structure unfolds into a multi-functional market stall, featuring a covered seating area with built-in chessboard and a stage on the roof for hosting events.

RAPHA MOBILE CYCLE CLUB

—

Designer
Wilson Brothers

Photographer
Jens Marott, Oscar Wilson

—

The Rapha Mobile Cycle Club is a unique combination of gallery, shop and café. A meeting place where riders can share their passion for road racing. In 2011, The Mobile Cycle Club visited a different event every week, including the Paris-Roubaix Challenge, the two Etape du Tour sportives, races in the UK and the World Championships in Copenhagen.

Wilson Brothers converted a 7.5 tonne truck to create the Mobile Cycle Club. The vehicle is equipped with a retractable awning, beneath which a set of six glazed-top oak and steel display tables house Rapha products, publications and ephemera. Together with six (stackable) benches, these double as café style tables from which to view race footage on a satellite-fed 60 inch TV screen whilst enjoying a coffee. An exterior display system, comprising a grid of ring-hooks fixed to the side of the vehicle, enables the Cycle Club environment to change the display at every stop, displaying special jerseys alongside framed photographs and race memorabilia.

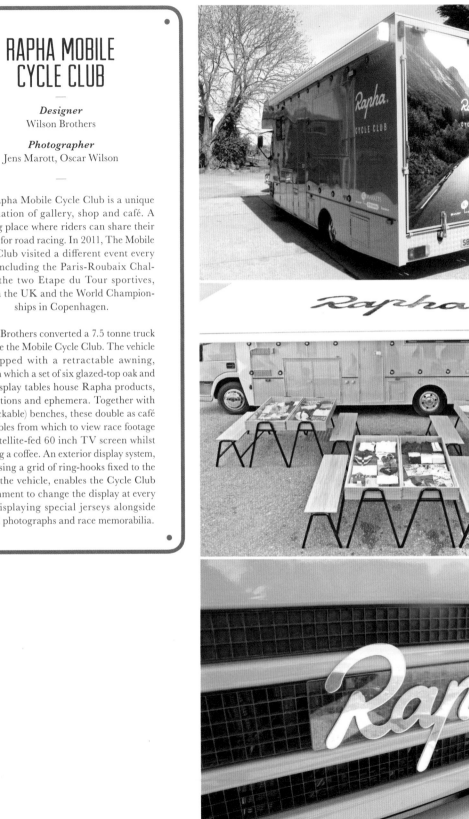

BEACH HOUSE

—

Designer
Re-Make/Re-Model

—

Beach House was a quick sketch and an entry in the Trailerpark festival architecture installation competition in 2011.

Sometimes you just want to go to the seaside. At this year's Trailerpark festival, we wanted to bring the fresh breeze of the beach to the concrete jungle. To do so, we simply slice the trailer in half, where one piece is transformed into a beach and the other half functions as the sea.

QTRAN – WORLD'S SMALLEST CARAVAN

Designer
Yannick Read

—

The QTran is designed to be towed behind a mobility scooter or bicycle. It is the world's smallest caravan.

CLASSROOM OF THE FUTURE

Client
London Borough
of Camden

***Structural
Engineer***
Michael Hadi
Associates

Services Engineer
ARUP

Fabrication
J.S.Fraser

Designer
Gollifer Langston
Architects

Photographer
James Brittain,
Gollifer Langston
Architects

A mobile expandable capsule designed to serve primary schools in a neighbourhood of London and to house special teaching facilities. The capsule arrives on the back of a lorry and can lower itself to the ground and expand—providing young pupils with an enticing environment in which to learn.

SOSH TRUCK

—

Designer
SOSH, ORANGE FRANCE

Photographer
David Turakiewicz, Pierre Dutilleux

—

The Sosh Truck is an authentic skate-board-ramp mounted on an American truck and covered with the brand's graphic identity. The truck drove to several places in Paris on September 20th and 21th 2013, such as the University Campus in the South, Tour Eiffel, Place de la Concorde, La Vilette.

French pro-skater and member of Sosh Riding Team, Sam Partaix, was the official ambassador of the whole operation. According to him and the crew he invited during the event, riding a tuck-mounted ramp in Paris was a once-in-a-lifetime experience. Through the project, Sosh highlighted that one does not need to live next to a skatepark to skate. The purpose of Sosh's commitment is to help action sports achieve a global audience and passion through ridesessions.com, a blog dedicated to ride culture.

MADE OUT PORTUGAL TRUCK GALLERY

Studio
Made Out Portugal

—

Made Out Portugal Truck Gallery was a exhibition set-up, designed and developed specifically for the DMY International Design Festival in Berlin 2011. During that time, the selected designers were based in Holland, leading us to solve the problem of transporting the projects to Berlin.

It was clear for us to use a movable exhibition concept as a solution, featuring the Made Out Platform concept to promote Portuguese designers abroad. The truck was rented from a Dutch rental company and was transformed into a gallery that could be on the move. Once the transformation was completed, we filled the truck, drove to Berlin's Tempelhof Airport, opened the truck's back door, and we were ready for the opening.

BLACK BOX REVELATION

Client	***Lighting Design***
Trailerpark Festival and S-tog	Christian Wolf (ClubVisuals.net), Re-Make/Re-Model
Architects	
Re-Make/Re-Model	***Construction***
	Re-Make/ Re-Model, Arjen Ulrich
Collaborating Architects	
Max Dengler, Victor Serrander, Anders Grivi Norman	***Photographer***
	Johanne Fick, Kenneth Nguyen, Nicolai Levin

At last summer's Copenhagen's Trailerpark Festival, a caravan was converted into a multi-purpose meeting space that was dark by day and night. Designers Anders G. Norman, Max Dengler and Victor Serrander cut away one side of the caravan and pushed the rest of it into a 6-by-6m black painted plywood box. Festival-goers were invited to enter the space and play with control buttons, changing the lighting and sound from subdued to bright and buzzing. The space was lit by spotlights and holes cut in the ceiling, which represented stars or lights of a city's skyline.

"The imprint of the caravan is the only entrance into the internal space," Norman says. "By making the bright trailer the entrance point and the control station where you can adjust the lights and sounds inside the black box, a connection is created between the two worlds: the colourful life of the festival outside and the mysterious creative world inside."

WOLF FM

Designer
Bureau Detours

Photographer
Bureau Detours La Familia

WOLF FM is Bureau Detours' tool for experimenting with the radio medium, by producing ultra local radio in the public space and hacking their way into peoples' living rooms. By doing this, Bureau Detours expand the reach of their public space experiments to new users. WOLF FM uses a custom-built pull cart as its mobile FM broadcasting unit, and the radio shows are mostly improvised with the participation of people dropping by. The mobility of the radio station enables WOLF FM to alter the public space in surprising ways, by not only working with the physical space but also the auditory space on-the-go.

WOLF FM by Bureau Detours took part in the Icelandic festival LungA in Seyðisfjörður, a festival of collaborative creativity.

ROLLING HUTS

Architect
Olson Kundig Architects

Project Team
Tom Kundig (FAIA, Design Principal), Jerry Garcia (Project Manager)

Contractor
Tim Tanner

Consultant
MCE Structural Consultants

The Rolling Huts are low-tech and low-impact in their design, and they sit lightly on their 40 acre site—a floodplain meadow in an alpine river valley. The owner purchased this former RV campground with the aim of building several guest huts for friends and allowing the landscape to return to its natural state, but zoning restrictions did not permit permanent structures to be built on the site. Kundig's witty, delightful solution was to put the huts on wheels, which lift the structures above the meadow, providing space for native grasses to grow while yielding unobstructed views of the surrounding mountains.

The construction of each hut is simple. It is, in essence, an offset, steel-clad box on a steel and wood platform. Walls are topped by clerestory windows, over which a SIPs panel roof floats in an inverted, lopsided V. At the north end, a double-paned sliding glass door opens to the outside and a covered deck. Interior finishes (cork and plywood) are unassuming, inexpensive, and left as raw as possible. Exteriors are made from durable materials (steel, plywood, and tongue-and-groove car decking) and require no-maintenance. The rustic character of the materials responds to the natural setting.

The six huts are grouped as a herd: while each is sited toward a view of the mountains (and away from the other structures), their proximity unites them. Showers and a parking area are located in and near the centrally located barn, a short distance from the herd. Rain and snowmelt from each hut are allowed to run off into the ground. The huts evoke Thoreau's simple cabin in the woods—structures that take second place to nature.

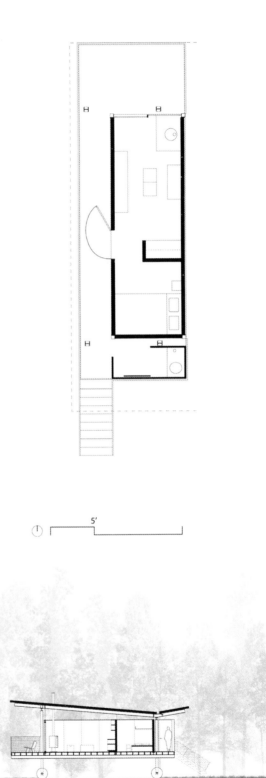

5'

Long Section

0   5'   15'   30'

NOTREE HOUSE

Designer
Ed Swan

Created during studies at the Royal College of Art, the NoTree House is a "tree house" for the urban environment. A contemplative and playful place, or just an escape from the mundane, familiar and hard uninviting city surroundings. Aimed at all ages, the NoTree House was designed for modern living where access to any tress are limited to looking at small gardens, back yards or concrete landscapes.

The intention of the project was to produce a tree house-like experience inside through the control of views and manipulation of light that comes into the space. It was important that these effects were of low-tech input, but producing a façade of hi-tech output, the unit was self-sufficient, needing nothing more from the surrounding environment.

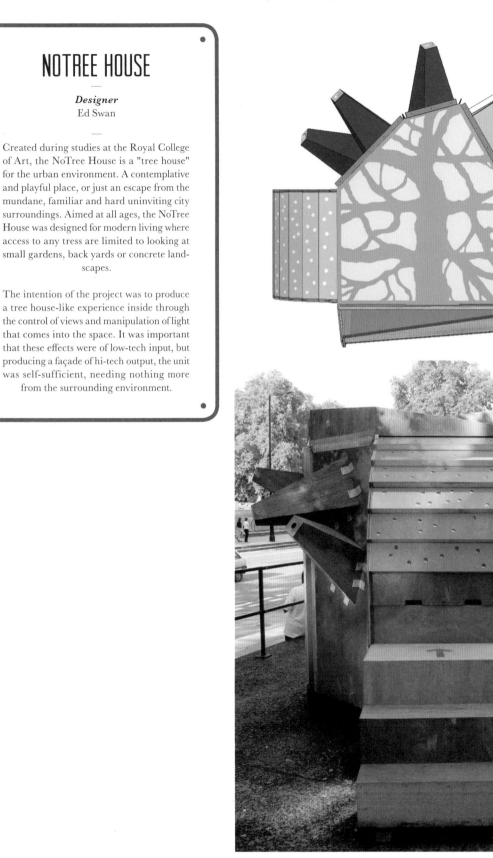

BEERHORST
WONDER WAGON

—

Designer
Beerhorst Family, GeoSpace Studio

—

The Wonder Wagon is the Beerhorst Family's Mobile Gallery made of recycled and repurposed material. It is pulled by hand to art markets and festivals. The wagon extends the ability of the family to reach potential customers by creating an iconic object that provides a memorable identity for the family. Most of the time it is parked in their driveway on a busy street where it acts as an unmanned storefront, selling cards and small crafts with a pay box attached to the inside wall.

FOLDING SAUNA

Designer
Elmo Vermijs

Technical Drawings
Studio Elmo Vermijs

Realisation
Elmo Vermijs,
Quinten Corbey,
Gerbrand Dros,
Roos Smith, Esmée
Thomassen

Photographer
Tessa Persijn

The Folding Sauna is an autonomous art project, inspired by the thought of bringing people together in public locations to enjoy a sauna session. By combining a trailer and a tent, the studio has created the main idea and starting point for this exciting concept.

EXILE

Studio
Vincench Studio

Photographer
Jose Angel Vincench Barrera

Collaboration
Jose Angel Vincench Barrera

"Exile" is an art installation composed of five mobile homes, each taking on the form of one of the letters used to spell out the word. The large-scale work is pretty self-explanatory—the empty trailers stand uninhabited and refer to individuals who are living outside of their own country for a particular reason; not necessarily because of a political situation, but also personal reasons, often existing in a state of isolation.

UNREAL ESTATE HOUSE

Studio
Van Bo Le-Mentzel

Collaboration
Wolfgang Ramisch

Photographer
Benjamin Heck

A wooden DIY cabin installed on car trailers. It has two floors; in the first floor (4 sqm), you find a kitchen, a toilet and office facilities, while upstairs is the sleeping area (2 sqm). The big foldable window is perfect for entertainment, retail or art purposes. During the winter period, it serves as a temporary home for homeless people.

CARAVAN 01 / CARAVAN 02

—

Designer
Kevin van Braak

Photographer
Leo van Kampen

—

My caravan appears to be no different from any other caravan when it is pulled behind a car. When opened, it manifests itself as an artificial garden, park or camping sight. Inside the caravan, there are stuffed animals, artificial grass silk flowers and trees, a sound installation with bird sounds and a BBQ pit.

COOLHAUS

—

Designer
Natasha Case, Freya Estreller

Photographer
Jolie Ruben for Time Out
NYC, Laure Joliet

—

Coolhaus is an architecturally-inspired, gourmet dessert company known for its unique ice cream sandwiches, featuring flavours like Fried Chicken & Waffles ice cream, Bourbon Manhattan ice cream, and Olive Oil Rosemary Pine Nut cookies.

Coolhaus launched from one postal van, which was converted in to a chrome ice cream truck with a pink top and chrome rims in 2009 at the Coachella Music Festival, and has grown to a fleet of 11 trucks in Los Angeles, New York City, Austin and Dallas, one cart in Central Park (New York City), two stores in LA and a wholesale distribution business in 45 states.

'GOOD/BAD/UGLY' (2012)

Designer
Karl Philips

Photographer
Kristof Vranken / Z33, Stef Langmans

Three mobile living units—The Good, the Bad, and the Ugly—adopt the language and shape of outdoor billboards for advertising, to blend into and temporarily occupy the public space. Nomadic performers, whose livelihoods are supported by the sale of the advertising space that literally encapsules them, inhabit the modules.

BUURTBIOS

Studio
Studio Makkink & Bey

Photographer
Kevin Smeeing

—

As a spin-off from Utrecht Manifest in 2012 and a follow-up of Buurtbios Hoograven by Jolanda van Iersel, Studio Makkink & Bey decided to make a mobile cinema together with Brilliante Ideeën, Vrede van Utrecht and District Office Utrecht South.

Buurtbios Rotsoord is organized by local residents and can make a stop at any desired place to project a movie. This allows movies to be programmed so that they can connect to a specific event in the neighborhood, such as a parade or a neighborhood meeting. Locally shot films or interactive recordings can premiere at the location where they are most relevant. They also aim to make big blockbusters freely accessible to everyone. The neighborhood cinema also constructs and reinforces social structures, making them visible and establishing contact between local residents and the municipality, or possibly functioning as an extension of a music venue nearby.

On Friday July 6th 2012, the first film screening was shown on the back of the the Buurtbios truck at the empty Vicona terrain. About a 100 people watched the award winning film, The Artist, for free. They came with their own chairs, picnic rugs and food, where the free coffee, soda and popcorn was available.

THE ROCKET
WOOD-FIRED PIZZA

Studio
Whiskey Design

Creative Director
Matt Wegerer

Designers
Matt Wegerer,
Shelby Mathews,
Lauren Bowles

Copywriter
Drunk Copywriter

Photographer
Austin Walsh Studio,
David Fox

Official sources will tell you that a team of former aerospace engineers designed and built this craft using space-grade materials at a classified site in the Yuma Desert. But ever since The Rocket arrived on the streets of Phoenix, rumors have persisted that the powerful (ahem) foreign technology is the real force behind this cheese-melting, sauce-bubbling, dough-firing creation. The truth is that we may never know the secret behind The Rocket. But as long as it keeps slinging the freshest pizzas this side of Naples, we're happy to let the mystery live on.

TRANSPORTABLE SAUNA CYLINDER

Designer
H3T architekti

Photographer
H3T architekti

Having had positive experiences with our first mobile sauna, we looked to improve and better the design. We attempted to find an optimal surface area of the sauna and simplify its material composition. The construction details had to be improved too as they have to withstand the sometimes rough weather and unusual physical conditions.

The mobile sauna's special chassis, with independent spring-loaded wheels, is designed as a wooden supporting structure from bent wood. We cooperated with a specialist from the TON a.s. furniture company on the design. The case of the sauna is made from plywood sheets and multiwall polycarbonate sheets which were supplied by the firm Arla Plast AB. It is heated by a wood-fired stove. The sauna was designed for two people, but it can hold up to four if they don't mind being a little less comfortable.

MODIO, THE MOBILE STUDIO PROJECT

—

Designer
Atelier OPA Co.,Ltd,
Metropolitan University

—

Modio is a mobile studio using an Airstream. We made it for Tokyo Designer's week Exhibition 2009, as a mobile studio for Metropolitan University.

Prof. Suzuki loves Airstream trailers, so he imported this small Airstream from the US and remodeled it for this project. He had the body cut open into a "wing" that can open and close, and designed an air-framed roof for the exhibition area. This air roof, which can inflate in 30 seconds, reflects his perpetual theme of "Architectural furniture creating a space around its own object."

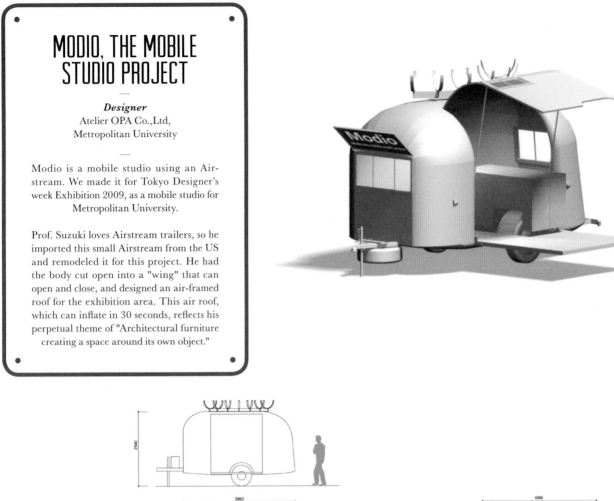

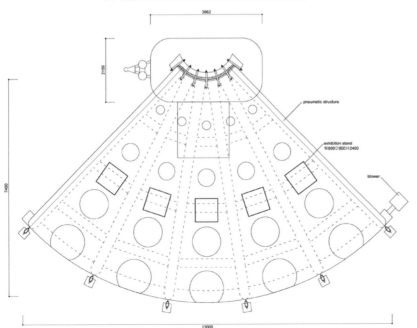

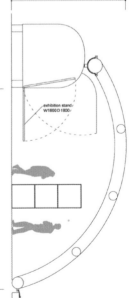

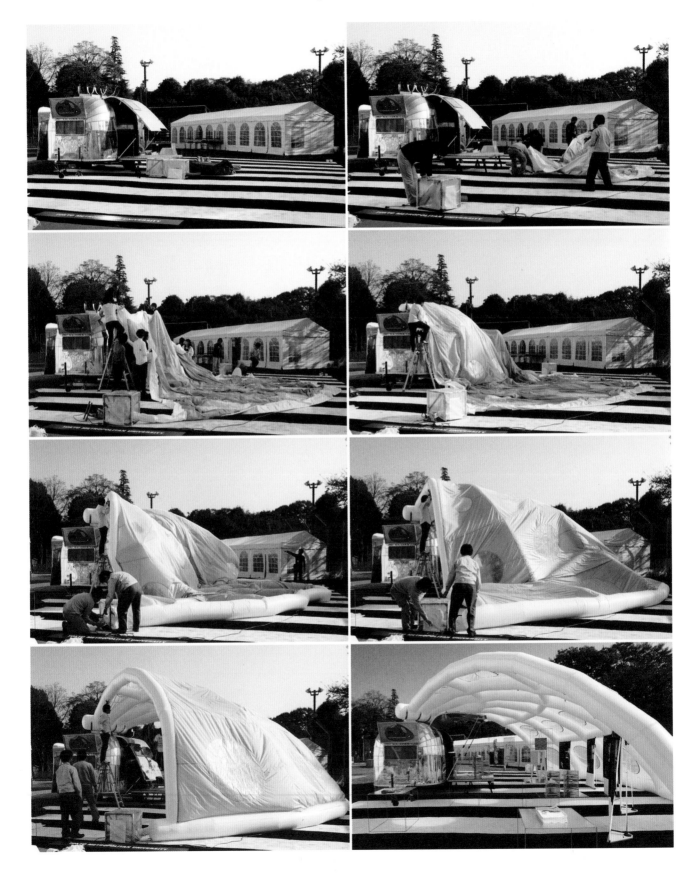

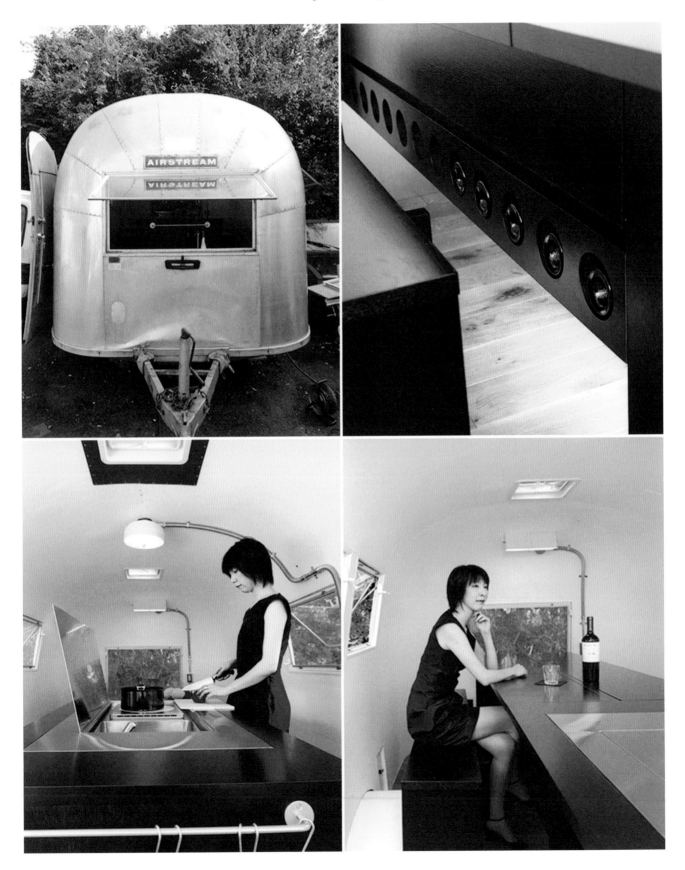

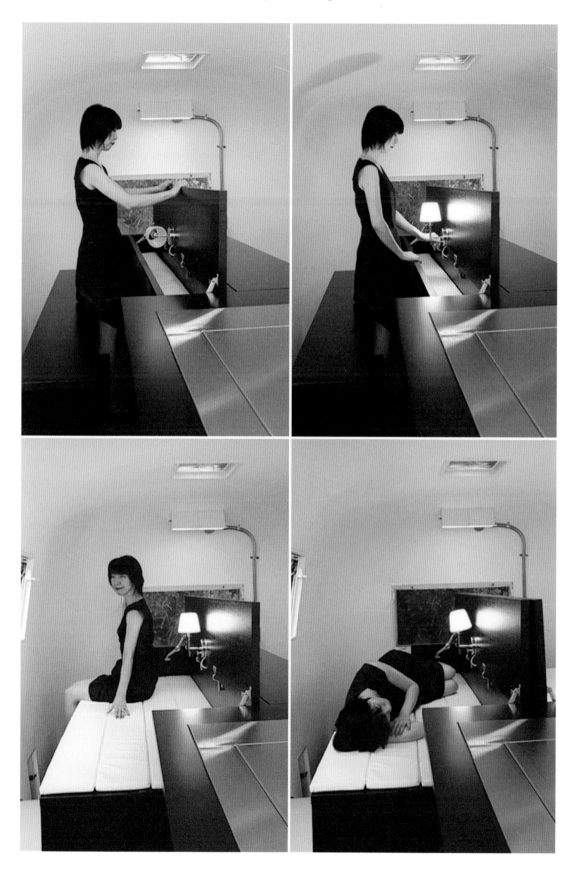

COLIM

—

Product Designer
Christian Susana

—

Colim is an acronym for Colours of Life in Motion. Colim is a car, caravan and camper, which is not only pleasing aesthetically, but has a handy detachable car for when you want to render the home element immobile...

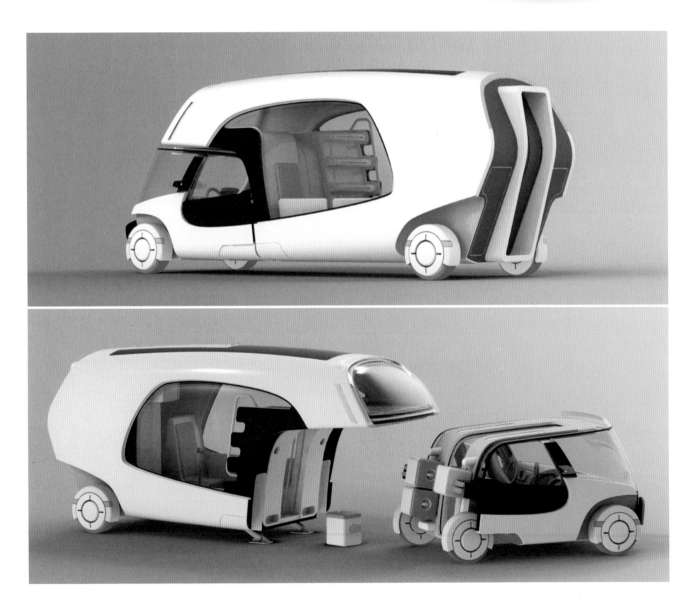

AIRSTREAM

—

Designer
Atelier OPA Co.,Ltd

Inside the trailer, I installed a long island based on kenchikukagu, which means "architectural furniture" and is the name of a collection of Kenchikukagu designs. The Kenchikukagu series Mobile Kitchen, Foldaway Office and Foldaway Guestroom are each housed in a wooden box that open or expands like an accordion to transform into a room that can later be rolled away. Likewise, the island in the middle of the Airstream unfolds to reveal an equipped kitchen as well as a dining table for six or two beds, each with its own reading light. The flexibility of the design adds to the longevity and the sustainability of the space.

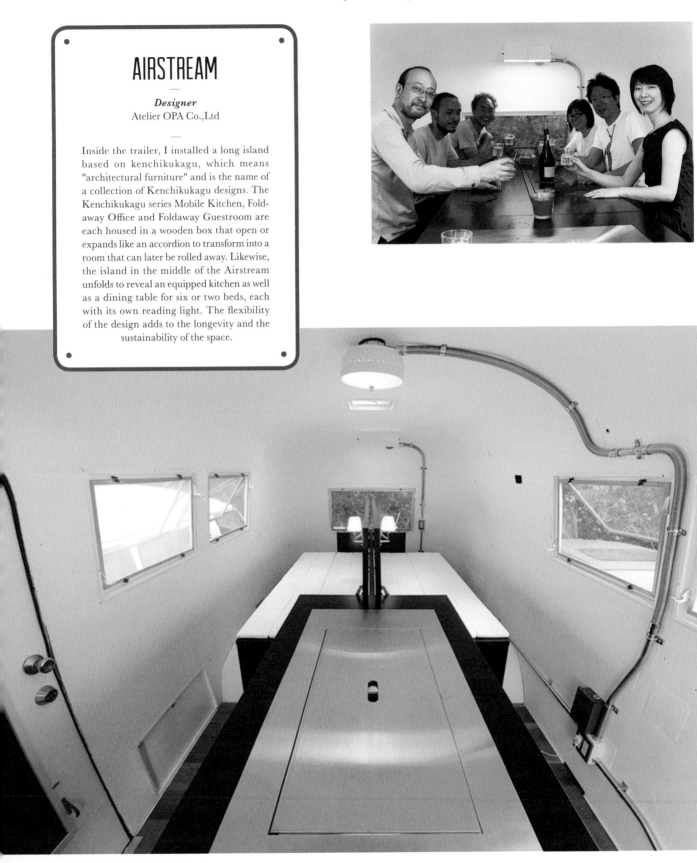

KENCHIKUKAGU in Airstream

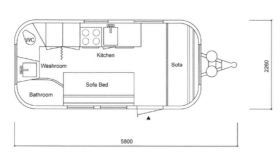

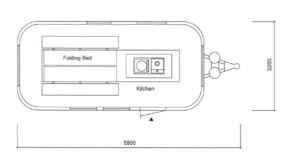

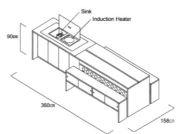

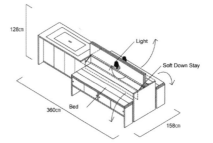

Open and shut structure : Soft Downstair
Material: Nara laminated lumber
Finishing: Urethane paint, Mat black
Open size: W 3600mm   D1500mm   H1410mm
Close size: W 3600mm   D1500mm   H1000mm
Equipment: Water system, Stainless sink, IH cooking heater, Two Foldaway beds, Two Bench
Occupant area: 4.28 square meters.
Order price: 1,200,000 JPN more (Airstream is not incluaed)

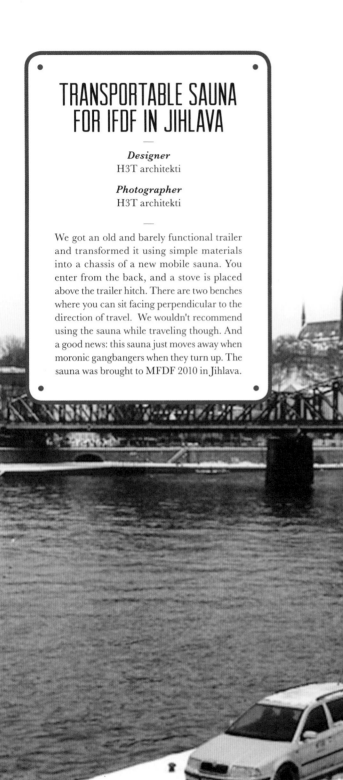

TRANSPORTABLE SAUNA FOR IFDF IN JIHLAVA

—

Designer
H3T architekti

Photographer
H3T architekti

—

We got an old and barely functional trailer and transformed it using simple materials into a chassis of a new mobile sauna. You enter from the back, and a stove is placed above the trailer hitch. There are two benches where you can sit facing perpendicular to the direction of travel. We wouldn't recommend using the sauna while traveling though. And a good news: this sauna just moves away when moronic gangbangers when they turn up. The sauna was brought to MFDF 2010 in Jihlava.

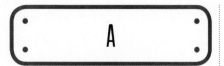

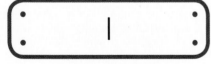

WHEEL AND DEAL

Idea and Concept by

Curated, Edited and Designed by

Working Title & Co.

First published and distributed in North America by Gingko Press

Published in 2015 by

Gingko Press, Inc
1321 Fifth Street
Berkeley, CA 94710
www.gingkopress.com

In association with

Basheer Graphic Books
Blk 13, Toa Payoh Lorong 8 #06-08,
Braddell Tech, Singapore 319261
Tel: +65 6336 0810 | Fax: +65 6259 1608
abdul@basheergraphic.com
www.basheergraphic.com

Idea and Concept © 2015 Basheer Graphic Books
Design and Editorial © 2015 Working Title & Co.
The copyright for individual text and design work is
held by the respective designers and contributors.

ISBN 978-1-58423-593-4

Printed and bound by

Tiger Printing (Hong Kong) Co. Ltd

Acknowledgements

We would like to thank all the designers and companies involved in the compilation of this book. This
project would not have been accomplished without their significant contribution. We would also like to
express our gratitude to all the producers for their invaluable opinions and assistance all this time. This
book's successful completion also owes a great deal to many professionals in the creative industry who
have provided precious insights and comments. Lastly to many others whose names, though not credited,
who have made a big impact on our work, we thank you for your continuous support the whole time.

Future Publications

If you would like to contribute to our future publications, please email us at
hello@workingtitleandco.com